Don M. Chance, CFA
Virginia Polytechnic Institute

Pamela P. Peterson, CFA
Florida State University

Real Options and Investment Valuation

The Research Foundation of AIMR™

Research Foundation Publications

Real Options and Investment Valuation

The Research Foundation of The Association for Investment Management and Research™, the Research Foundation of AIMR™, and the Research Foundation logo are trademarks owned by the Research Foundation of the Association for Investment Management and Research. CFA®, Chartered Financial Analyst™, AIMR-PPS®, and GIPS® are just a few of the trademarks owned by the Association for Investment Management and Research. To view a list of the Association for Investment Management and Research's trademarks and a Guide for the Use of AIMR's Marks, please visit our Web site at www.aimr.org.

ISBN 0-943205-57-3

Printed in the United States of America

July 2002

Editorial Staff
Maryann Dupes
Book Editor

Christine E. Kemper
Assistant Editor

Jaynee M. Dudley
Production Manager

Cheryl L.L. Montgomery
Production Coordinator

Kelly T. Bruton/Lois A. Carrier
Composition

Mission

The Research Foundation's mission is to encourage education for investment practitioners worldwide and to fund, publish, and distribute relevant research.

Biographies

Don M. Chance, CFA, is First Union Professor of Financial Risk Management at Virginia Tech. His research has appeared in academic and professional journals; has been presented at seminars, conferences and workshops in the United States and abroad; and has been funded by the Chicago Board of Trade and Research Foundation. He is associate editor of the *Journal of Derivatives*, the *Journal of Alternative Investments*, and the *Financial Review*. Professor Chance is the author of *An Introduction to Derivatives* (5th edition), *Essays in Derivatives*, and the forthcoming *Derivatives for the CFA Program*, which will be the standard derivatives text for the Chartered Financial Analysts Program. He has extensive experience as an instructor in professional development programs, a consultant, and a speaker before practitioner groups, and he was the founder of Virginia Tech's student-managed investment portfolio. Professor Chance has been cited or quoted in the financial media in print, online, and on television. Professor Chance holds a Ph.D. from Louisiana State University.

Pamela P. Peterson, CFA, is a professor of finance at Florida State University. She has taught at FSU since receiving her degree in 1981. Professor Peterson has published articles in journals including the *Journal of Finance*, the *Journal of Financial Economics,* the *Journal of Banking and Finance*, *Financial Management*, and the *Financial Analysts Journal*. Professor Peterson is the author of *Financial Management and Analysis*, co-author with David R. Peterson of the Research Foundation monograph *Company Performance and Measures of Value Added*, and co-author with Frank Fabozzi of *Analysis of Financial Statements* and *Capital Budgeting*. Professor Peterson holds a Ph.D. from the University of North Carolina.

Contents

Foreword

Real options deal with choices about real investments as opposed to financial investments. Although initially applied to mining, oil, and gas projects, real option valuation has since been expanded to address a wide range of managerial choices that affect a company's value. To many financial analysts, the presence of real options is not readily apparent, and even if they are known, most analysts are unclear about how to value such options. This failure leads analysts to incorrectly value companies, and often by a wide margin. With this excellent monograph, Don Chance and Pamela Peterson have produced an invaluable resource to help financial analysts recognize and value real options.

They begin by contrasting real option valuation with traditional discounted cash flow methods, and they demonstrate the added flexibility associated with real option valuation. Chance and Peterson next use binomial trees to illustrate the valuation of growth options, deferral options, and abandonment options. Growth options offer management the flexibility to expand the scale of a project. Deferral options enable management to commit quickly while postponing investment to a future date. Abandonment options grant management the flexibility to terminate further investment and to recover any salvage value.

Chance and Peterson use the continuous time Black–Scholes model to value the real options associated with Cisco Systems, and they show how real option valuation uncovers value that traditional methods overlook. They are careful, however, to present a balanced view of this important topic by discussing the many challenges associated with real option valuation. They describe, for example, that an increase in volatility raises the value of real options if other factors are held constant. A rise in volatility, however, may raise the discount rate and thus lower the value of the underlying asset, which, in turn, drives down the value of the option. They also point out that real options are not always independent of one another; hence, their values are not additive. Chance and Peterson underscore the fact that many of the underlying assumptions associated with option valuation are not literally true; to wit, returns are not necessarily random nor precisely lognormally distributed, and volatility is not known and constant. Moreover, valuing real options is usually more difficult than financial options because many of the input values, such as exercise price, discount rate, and time to expiration, are not as easily observable. Chance and Peterson are quick to point out, however, that the opaqueness of these values presents a similar challenge to those who rely on traditional valuation methods. They conclude with a review of the empirical research on the accuracy of real option valuation.

Even though real options do not appear on the balance sheet, anyone who is serious about asset valuation must be able to identify and value them. These critical tasks are now much easier thanks to Chance and Peterson's outstanding monograph. The Research Foundation is pleased to present *Real Options and Investment Valuation.*

Mark Kritzman, CFA
Research Director
The Research Foundation of the
Association for Investment Management and Research

Preface

Real options are opportunities that are associated with investment projects characterized by a degree of flexibility. Real options involve choices: to invest or not, to terminate or continue an investment, or to defer or carry on with an investment, to name a few. Real options can have considerable value, not only to the companies possessing them but also to the analysts examining those companies. Uncovering the value of real options is a challenging task.

The purpose of this monograph is to bridge the gap between theory and practice in the application of option valuation methods to capital investment projects and to make real options valuation more accessible and comprehensible to practicing financial analysts. A large body of published literature exists on real options. Some of it is technically quite complex. Much of it oversimplifies the hidden complexities of real options valuation. In this monograph, we bring to the analyst a consolidated and concise overview of the latest thinking from experts in real options, showing how these options are structured, how they should be valued, and how to apply the valuation models. In contrast to much of the published work on real options, we also provide a more critical analysis of the limitations of the models and the difficulties of using them.

The monograph is organized in the following manner. In Chapter 1, we provide a general introduction to the topic of valuing companies and a specific introduction to the topic of valuation techniques with an emphasis on real options valuation. In Chapter 2, we discuss the traditional approaches to dealing with optionable elements in an investment opportunity. We demonstrate how discounted cash flow analysis, decision tree analysis, sensitivity analysis, and simulation analysis address the flexibility options in an investment project. We also provide an example of how real options can be used in valuation applications beyond capital budgeting. Through examples and applications presented in Chapter 3, we then demonstrate a framework for how real options methods provide correct valuations in a variety of capital investment settings. Recognizing the many challenges to applying options methods to real asset investment opportunities, we demonstrate in Chapter 4 how to apply real options valuation to a start-up company that has a growth option. In Chapter 5, we discuss the limitations and difficulties of using real options, and we challenge the assumptions on which the models are based. In Chapter 6, we highlight some empirical evidence on the actual use of real options and the accuracy of the valuations of these options. In Chapter 7, we provide a capsule summary of the key findings and conclusions from this monograph.

Some of the terms and phrases in this monograph might be new or only vaguely familiar to some readers. Thus, to help with the comprehension of this subject, we have included a glossary at the end of the monograph. To denote a word or phrase found in the glossary, on first use it is given special type treatment. For example, in the following sentence, the phrase "real options valuation" is found in the glossary: "This process is referred to as **real options valuation**."

We would like to thank the Research Foundation of the Association for Investment Management and Research for its support in making this monograph possible. We especially appreciate the assistance, support, and encouragement of Research Director Mark Kritzman.

1. Introduction

Analyzing the investment potential of a publicly traded company is a challenging task. An analyst assembles a vast amount of information from a variety of sources, carefully avoiding inappropriate nonpublic information and ignoring information in the form of rumor rather than fact. Standard discounted cash flow (DCF) techniques are commonly applied to estimated future cash flows, leading to an overall assessed value of the company. The analyst must often probe not only the finances of a company but also the more subtle possibilities that a company may have for creating wealth, which is where the task gets really difficult. A good analyst uncovers the hidden value in a company. That hidden value may emanate from a variety of sources, but rarely, if ever, will it be easy to detect. Perhaps the difficulty in uncovering hidden value is fortunate, for if it were easy to detect, then in all likelihood, it would already be built into the current market value. And detecting that hidden value before everyone else is what good analysis is all about.

Although investment analysts rarely delve into the micro level of analyzing specific projects of companies, they must understand how companies themselves value their own investment projects. Some companies make value-enhancing capital investments; others make poor capital investments. Understanding how companies make capital investments is important to an investment analyst looking at a company as an outsider.

The DCF approach to valuation is an important tool in the analysis of a capital investment. The valuation of an investment in physical or real assets typically focuses on a series of fixed future cash flows that are expected to be generated from this investment. Whether valuing a single project or an entire business enterprise, the valuation process is generally the same—estimate future incremental cash flows, discount these flows to the present using the appropriate project cost of capital, and compare the present value of these cash flows with the present value of the investment outlays. Although this approach is generally well accepted, in many instances the DCF approach does not capture the realistic valuation of an investment. Many investments in real assets have opportunities, such as abandonment, expansion, and deferment, that may alter the investment's future cash flows and thus its value. These options generally involve the flexibility to revise decisions in the future; hence, they are often referred to as **flexibility options**.

Consider the valuation of a technology company that has exclusive rights to patents on software that is not yet in the market. Using the DCF approach, the analyst would attempt to estimate the future cash flows that may result when any products using these patents are brought to market. But missing from the DCF analysis is the ability to capture the flexibility that this company has, for example, to delay bringing the products to market, to expand or contract production once the products are brought to the market, and to abandon production. And this flexibility is valuable. Moreover, this flexibility is often subtle, if not hidden, and unrecognized by others. Investment analysts should, therefore, understand how companies identify and analyze these types of situations.

To properly analyze such opportunities, traditional methods of valuing investments, such as DCF, should be supplemented with an approach that applies option-pricing methods to the valuation of capital investments in real assets. This process is referred to as **real options valuation**. The importance of real options valuation arises from the fact that traditional methods of valuation do not directly consider the managerial flexibility available in many investment decisions and hence tend to understate the value of investments. Thus, some of a company's value can be derived from options that simply do not show up on financial statements.

Real options valuation does not replace traditional DCF methods. Indeed, DCF techniques play an important role in the identification of real options and provide input information for real options valuation. But whereas many analysts are aware of the importance of incorporating option value in their analysis of an investment, most lack an understanding of how to incorporate option valuation into the decision process. For example, Busby and Pitts (1997), in their survey of FTSE 100 companies, found that although most companies are aware of the importance of flexibility options, most do not have procedures for explicitly incorporating these options in the decision process.[1] In turn, investment analysts, observing a company from the outside, also lack an understanding of the role these options play in assessing the overall value of the company.

Of course, most companies do not possess just one real option. Most have a variety of different capital investments and many options. This multiplicity of oftentimes interrelated options makes valuing a company and its opportunities even harder. But regardless of the difficulty, good analysis requires that one face this challenge. And in this day and age when the market's valuation of companies, especially technology and Internet-related companies, often

---

[1]We discuss this study in more detail in Chapter 5.

differs significantly from that predicted by traditional valuation methods, such as DCFs, P/Es, and dividend valuation models, understanding real options is all the more important.

Real Options in the Technology Sector

Nowhere is the effect of real options on company valuation more apparent than in the Internet and technology sectors. Consider the valuation of Amazon.com, an online retailer. This company has generated losses each year since beginning business in 1995, and it is not expected to generate a profit at least until 2003. Cash flows are not positive and are not expected to be positive for a number of years hence. Despite these bleak financial results, its stock has traded as high as $113 per share. When Amazon was trading around $64 per share, a little more than half of that value could be attributed to its cash flows, with at least a part of the remainder attributed to numerous options to expand into different but related markets.[2]

Amazon's situation is similar to one discussed in Dunbar (2000). The Real Options Group, a London-based consulting firm, applied real options pricing to value Tiscali, an Internet service provider start-up, and determined that the value of the company exceeded its DCF because of the company's options to earn revenues through growth in Europe and through growth in the mobile phone market. Although young, start-up technology companies with little or no earnings histories may be difficult to value and can be overvalued by investors based on market hype, cases exist of large companies with established earnings, such as Cisco Systems, that are valued by investors outside the bounds of traditional valuation "yardsticks."[3]

Valuation information as of July 28, 2000, for a sampling of companies in both the computer services and computer hardware industries is provided in **Table 1.1**. Industry averages and the average for the S&P 500 Index are also provided in this table. Although some companies have valuations that are in line with those of the traditional valuation indicators (for example, IBM's P/E of 25.1 is in line with the S&P 500's P/E of 25.0), several of the companies in this table have valuations that are outside traditional reasonable valuation bounds, such as CNET Networks, Lycos, and Yahoo!.

---

[2]This and other examples of actual valuations in this monograph are written from the perspective of the end of the year 2000 and will, of course, be out of date by the time the monograph is printed. The principles that we are illustrating, however, will not be out of date.

[3]See Pulliam (2000) for the example of Cisco and a discussion of the extent to which its P/E and PEG (i.e., price–earnings to growth) relations are out of line with traditional valuation. We take a closer look at Cisco and Amazon and provide further comments about their real options in Chapter 4.

Table 1.1. Current Valuation of Selected Companies as of July 28, 2000

Company	Price per Share	52-Week Low Price	52-Week High Price	Sales per Share[a]	Book Value per Share[b]	EPS[a]	This Year EPS Estimate	Next Year EPS Estimate	EPS Growth Next 5 Years	Beta	P/E[a]	PEG[c]	P/B[b]	Market Cap (billions)	Analysts' Opinion (Δ)
Computer services															
America Online	$ 53.813	$38.469	$ 53.813	$ 2.64	$ 2.67	$0.48	$0.57	$0.80	48.4%	2.51	142.4	3.79	20.19	$123.6	1.5
CNET	28.125	21.205	79.875	1.95	15.17	3.94	0.14	0.54	46.3	1.06	213.3	na	1.85	2.1	1.5
Lycos	58.063	28.563	93.625	2.44	13.47	0.20	0.18	0.55	49.3	3.02	333.9	na	4.31	6.4	1.9
Yahoo!	126.750	55.000	250.063	1.39	2.98	0.33	0.46	0.58	46.3	3.45	291.0	3.61	42.48	68.9	1.6
Industry									51.2		−10.1	−0.27			
Computer hardware															
Cisco Systems	62.813	28.078	82.000	2.32	2.86	0.35	0.53	0.70	31.9	1.45	128.2	3.24	177.94	441.2	1.3
Dell Computer Corp.	43.688	35.000	59.688	9.90	2.17	0.64	0.92	1.21	30.8	1.96	49.5	1.39	20.11	113.0	1.5
Gateway	55.125	36.563	84.000	27.63	7.28	1.51	1.85	2.27	23.8	0.80	31.2	0.90	7.57	17.7	1.4
IBM	111.813	89.000	111.813	86.30	10.87	3.94	4.39	4.99	13.8	1.11	25.1	1.41	10.29	198.2	1.4
Sun Micro-systems	102.813	32.938	110.000	9.30	4.60	1.09	1.27	1.57	22.1	1.26	111.9	5.00	22.37	163.5	1.6
Industry									26.7		50.9	9.25			
S&P 500									12.1		25.0	1.81			

Note: Δ = Average among brokers, with 1 = strong buy and 5 = strong sell.

[a] Based on trailing 12 months.
[b] Based on most recent quarter.
[c] Ratio of price per share to the most recent earnings growth rate.

Source: Yahoo! Finance.

Another example is Yahoo!, a well-known provider of Web services. Yahoo! stock has traded at a P/E of almost 300 times historical earnings. Unlike some Internet-related companies, Yahoo! has generated positive earnings, and its earnings are expected to grow at a rate of 46.3 percent over the next five years (2000–2005). But even with these projected earnings, the current value of the stock far exceeds traditional measures of valuation.[4] For example, using the average P/E for the S&P 500 of 25.0, the market cap of Yahoo! is estimated to be $5.9 billion, well below the $68.9 billion actual value.[5]

So, what do Amazon and Yahoo! have that is valued so highly? The current valuation is not based on historical performance, and it does not appear to be based on near-term performance. In the case of Amazon, the company is a leader in online retailing and has established a significant share of the online retail book market. Being a step ahead in terms of technology and marketing strategies online has helped it gain attention and customer loyalty and has allowed the company to branch out into nonbook markets as well. So, what does Amazon have? The opportunity to grow not only within its current markets but, more importantly, in new markets that leverage its existing infrastructure and customer base. Does any guarantee exist that Amazon will be able to capitalize on its present position? No, and evaluating the potential rewards and the uncertainties associated with these rewards is difficult. Customer loyalty can be fickle, the company has significant debt obligations, and technology changes quite rapidly. The first-mover advantage can create short-term value added, but the ease of entry into the online market, as seen recently by the traditional "bricks-and-mortar" companies, makes this advantage quite tenuous. In the case of Yahoo!, whose revenues are primarily from advertising, the company established itself as a portal to the Web and has added services, such as auction sites, that expand from its portal existence. So, what does Yahoo! have? The opportunity to grow and, as noted above, to leverage its current operations into new activities. Does any guarantee exist that Yahoo! will be able to capitalize on its present position as a leading portal that garners significant "hits"? No. The barriers to entry into the portal market are quite low, and technology and tastes change rapidly in this market.

Traditional valuation models that use current and projected earnings and cash flows do not fully capture the potential growth that is not reflected in current and projected earnings and cash flows. Some, such as Schwartz and

---

[4]Based on the 2000 fiscal year's earnings and the expected five-year growth rate, the P/E is more than 90.

[5]To illustrate the dramatic change in valuations over time for Internet companies, consider that the market capitalization of Yahoo! was $8.77 billion in May 2002; this amount represents a fall-off in value of more than 87 percent since 2000.

Moon (2000), have argued that given sufficiently high growth rates and high volatility, the valuations of some of these companies can be explained using real options. And some, such as Mayor (2001), argue that real options cannot explain some of the most extreme market valuations relative to DCFs. Furthermore, some have observed that the extraordinary valuations persist for only the larger companies in their respective technology-based industries.[6] These examples and more raise the question of whether the market is incorporating other factors, such as growth options, into the values of the stocks of these companies. These extraordinary valuations have challenged analysts to revise their traditional valuation "yardsticks." Unless analysts and investors are misvaluing companies to an almost unheard-of degree, real options almost surely explain a portion of the high values seen in some of these companies.[7] Of course, how much real options can account for the seemingly excessive valuations of companies is difficult to judge, but without an understanding of real options, one might attribute all of an apparent misvaluation to excessive optimism.

Background and Methodology of Real Options

Real options inherent in capital investment have long been acknowledged. For example, Myers (1977) recognized the importance of considering investment opportunities as growth options, and Kester (1984) emphasized the importance of growth options in investment decision making. Only recently, however, has much attention been paid to actually applying the valuation methods of option-pricing theory to real options. The "bottom line" of real options in capital investment is managerial flexibility; every investment project presents some degree of flexibility in decision making. The first challenge is recognizing the options inherent in investment decisions. The second challenge is to value these options and incorporate them into the valuation process.

The term "real options" apparently came into being with the 1977 work of Myers, in which he breaks down the value of a company into two components—the present value of assets in place and the present value of future growth opportunities.[8] The vast majority of the early academic research in real options following Myers's work focused on the mining and

---

[6]This observation was first made by Michael Mauboussin, chief investment strategist for Credit Suisse First Boston, as reported by Ip (1999).

[7]The revision of P/Es by analysts to fit current valuations of some companies is reported by Pulliam.

[8]This breakdown is similar to that used by Leibowitz (1997), in which the value of the firm is broken down into two components—the tangible value from existing assets and the value derived from new investments.

oil and gas industries. Over time, researchers have explored different options inherent in investment decisions, including the abandonment option, the flexibility to switch, the option to enter and exit, the right to defer, and the option to exploit successive innovations. A listing of many of the studies on real options is provided in **Exhibit 1.1**. The typical options inherent in an investment opportunity include the option to abandon, the option to expand or grow, the option to defer investment, and the option to change by altering the mix of production or use of the capital assets.

Consider the following two examples that appeared in print recently. Stonier (2001) describes the options inherent in the sales contracts of Airbus Industrie. Aircraft sales contracts include many options for the customer— the option to wait to sign a sales contract, the option for delivery (specific time), and the option to switch aircraft. Michaels (2000) reports that Air France has a nonreported asset whose value is derived from its ability to expand at Charles de Gaulle Airport in Paris. Of course, the French air transport industry does not have a monopoly on real options; they appear everywhere. Real options methodology has been applied to value lease contracts and to the management of foreign currency exposure, among other uses.[9] Even something as general and as broad as corporate strategy has been described as a "portfolio of real options" that cannot be adequately valued using the traditional net present value approach.[10]

So, how does an analyst take into account the values of these options? One approach is to use either **sensitivity analysis** or **simulation analysis** to analyze the available opportunities. Although these methods allow a look at the possible outcomes of a decision, they do not provide guidance regarding which course of action—of the many—to take. Another approach is the use of **decision tree** analysis, associating probabilities with each of the possible outcomes for an event and mapping out the possible outcomes and the value of the investment opportunity associated with these different outcomes. Although sensitivity analysis, simulation analysis, and decision tree analysis offer some assistance in capturing flexibility, an option-pricing framework provides an approach to analysis that is richer and more comprehensive.[11]

---

[9] See Grenadier (1995) for his presentation of the valuation of lease contracts using real options, Capel (1997) for an analysis of using a real options approach to manage foreign currency exposure, Mayers (1998) for evidence on firms' matching of real options and financial options, and Grenadier (1996) for an application to real estate development.

[10] See Luehrman (1998b) for a discussion of the inadequacy of DCF approaches to valuing corporate strategy. The role of real options in providing insight into corporate strategy is discussed by Triantis (1999).

[11] We examine each of these methods in Chapter 2.

Exhibit 1.1. Studies in Real Options

Option Type	Description	Studies
Abandonment	The option to stop use of the assets, realizing the salvage value.	Bonini (1977); Myers and Majd (1990); Berger, Ofek, and Swary (1996)
Flexibility to switch	The option to alter output or input mixes in response to changes in demand or prices.	Kulatilaka (1988, 1993); Kulatilaka and Marcus (1988); Triantis and Hodder (1990); Kulatilaka and Trigeorgis (1994)
Enter and exit	The option to exit an investment activity and re-enter as conditions become more favorable.	Robichek and Van Horne (1967); Brennan and Schwartz (1985); McDonald and Siegel (1985); Trigeorgis and Mason (1987); Pindyck (1988); Dixit (1989, 1992); Majd and Pindyck (1989); Myers and Majd
Right to defer	The option to delay investment outlays until such time that the investment is more profitable.	Tourinho (1979); Titman (1985); McDonald and Siegel (1986); Majd and Pindyck (1987); Paddock, Siegel, and Smith (1988); Pindyck (1991, 1993); Ingersoll and Ross (1992); Quigg (1993); Østbye (1997)
Staged investment	The option to make investment outlays in successive stages with the right to abandon the project as more information becomes available.	Roberts and Weitzman (1981); Majd and Pindyck (1987); Carr (1988); Trigeorgis (1993a); Grenadier (1996)
Growth	The option to capitalize on an earlier investment, such as one in research and development, to enter into related investment projects.	Myers (1977); Kester (1984, 1993); Trigeorgis (1988); Pindyck (1988); Chung and Charoenwong (1991); Kemna (1993); Brealey and Myers (1996); Grenadier and Weiss (1997); Chatwin, Bonduelle, Goodchild, Harmon, and Mazzuco (1999)
Interacting options	Multiple options, including the option to defer, to expand, to switch.	Trigeorgis (1991, 1993a, 1993b); Childs, Ott, and Triantis (1998)

The basic idea of real options valuation is to consider that the value of an investment extends beyond its value as measured by traditional DCFs or net present value (NPV). In other words, the value of a project is supplemented by the value of its options. Because the options are considered strategic decisions, the revised or supplemented NPV is referred to as the **strategic NPV**. Consider an investment opportunity that has one option associated with

8

it. The strategic NPV is the sum of the traditional NPV, which we call the **static NPV**, and the value added of the option analysis:

Strategic NPV = Static NPV + Value added of the option analysis.

Like options on financial assets, a real option can be a **call option**, which is the option to buy an asset, or a **put option**, which is the option to sell an asset. Like other options, a real option can be an **European option**, which is an option that can be exercised only on a specific date, or an **American option**, which is an option that can be exercised at any time on or before a specific date. In some cases, a real option can be in the form of an option to exercise another option, which is referred to as a **compound option**.

All options are characterized by an underlying asset, such as a stock or foreign currency, and permit the right to buy (if a call) or sell (if a put) the underlying asset at a fixed price. That price is called the **exercise price**, which is also sometimes called the strike price. Options have a finite life: They expire on a specific date, and either on that date or before (if an American option), a decision is made whether to exercise the option.[12] When the holder of a call option exercises it, the exercise price is paid and the underlying asset is acquired; when the holder of a put option exercises it, the underlying asset is delivered and the exercise price is received.

Determining an option's value is a task that requires the use of theoretical models. Under certain assumptions, the valuation of an option is obtained by a formula developed by Black and Scholes (1973) and Merton (1973). The formula's impact on the financial industry has been tremendous and has led to the growth of a large market in financial options and other derivatives. It is probably safe to say that this is the most widely applied theoretical model in the entire financial world. In recognition of the tremendous contribution of the model, Scholes and Merton received the 1997 Nobel Prize in economics for their role in its discovery. Black, who had died in 1995, was ineligible for the award but is widely recognized as a major contributor. Normally referred to as the **Black–Scholes model**, its derivation is technically quite complex, but its basic structure is simple. This formula relates five factors to the option's value:

P = the underlying asset's price,

X = the strike (exercise) price of the option,

r = the continuously compounded risk-free rate of interest,

σ = volatility (i.e., standard deviation) of the asset's return, and

T = the time to expiration in years.

---

[12]Unlike financial options, which have specific expiration dates, the expiration dates of real options may not be well defined, a point we shall discuss in Chapter 5.

Mapping the factors that affect the value of a stock option to those that affect the value of a real option, we see that we can capture the value of a real option much as we have with an option on a financial asset, as shown in **Exhibit 1.2**.

Although we shall look at the use of this model in more detail in Chapters 2, 4, and 5, consider a simple example, the option to abandon. In this case, the underlying asset consists of the continuing operations, so the value of the underlying asset is the value associated with the operations. The strike or exercise price for this option is the **exit value** or **salvage value** of the asset. The time to expiration is a measure of the time remaining until the option expires. So, at some point, the option will no longer be available. This point may well be at the end of the usable life of the underlying operations, or it may be earlier. The risk-free rate is the interest rate on an alternative but risk-free investment that matures at the time the option expires. The risk-free rate represents the opportunity cost. The volatility is a reflection of the variability or uncertainty of whether the option will ultimately have value. These variables enter into the Black–Scholes formula to provide the value of the option. Of course, as we shall see, the Black–Scholes formula is not always (perhaps, even rarely) the best approach to take to value real options, but it is the foundation on which most option valuation techniques rest.

Exhibit 1.2. Relating Financial Options to Real Options

Parameter	Option on a Financial Asset	Option on a Real Asset
P	The stock's price	The present value of cash flows from the investment opportunity (e.g., cash-out price)
X	The strike (exercise) price of the option	The present value of the delayed capital expenditure or future cost savings
r	The risk-free rate of interest	The continuously compounded risk-free rate of interest
σ	Volatility of the stock's return	The volatility (i.e., standard deviation of the project's relative value)[a]
T	The time to expiration in years	The option's life

[a]In standard option-pricing analysis, the volatility measures the volatility of the continuously compounded rate of return on the underlying asset. In applying option valuation procedures to real options, we must, therefore, interpret the volatility as the volatility of the relative value (i.e., the period-to-period percentage change in the value). See Chapters 4 and 5 for more on volatility.

Many challenges arise when applying option valuation methods to options on real assets. These challenges include identifying the many options within an investment, estimating volatility, and dealing with interacting options. We look at these challenges in the chapters that follow.

Summary

Real options valuation provides a method of incorporating managerial flexibility into investment decisions. Although such approaches as decision tree analysis offer a way of incorporating options into decision making, real options valuation provides a more comprehensive means of incorporating flexibility options. The complexity of real options valuation, however, does present some challenges. In the next chapter, we will look at traditional valuation models and then introduce real options valuation models to set the groundwork for the real options analyses and discussion that will follow in later chapters.

2. Valuation Models: Traditional versus Real Options

The valuation of an investment opportunity normally focuses on a series of future cash flows that are expected from this opportunity. The typical process of evaluating an investment opportunity involves estimating future cash flows, discounting these cash flows to the present at a rate that reflects the risk of the project, and comparing this discounted value of these cash flows with the required investment outlay. If the investment is expected to create value—that is, the present value of these future cash flows exceeds the investment outlay—the project is desirable; otherwise, the company will not make the investment.

When managers estimate what it costs to invest in a given project and what its benefits will be in the future, they are coping with uncertainty. The uncertainty arises from different sources, depending on the type of investment being considered, as well as the circumstances and the industry in which it is operating. Uncertainty can result from economic factors, market conditions, taxes, and interest rates, among many other sources.

These sources of uncertainty influence future cash flows. Thus, managers need to assess the uncertainty associated with a project's cash flows in order to select value-adding projects. One of the challenges in evaluating an investment opportunity is capturing the flexibility options that a project offers. An approach to dealing with these flexibility options is to use traditional methods that have been developed and used to capture some of the uncertainty that a project contains. Another approach is to value the project with option-pricing methods. We will first take a look at the traditional tools, such as discounted cash flow (DCF) and decision tree analysis, and then we shall take a look at how option pricing can help value investment opportunities. These tools will be illustrated by using the following investment opportunity.

Investment Opportunity for the Hokie Company

The Hokie Company is evaluating whether or not to invest in research and development (R&D). Initially, only two choices exist—to invest $10 million in R&D or not to invest in R&D. But the investment in R&D is only the beginning. The outcome of the R&D is uncertain:

The research may yield a product or not. A 70 percent chance exists that the R&D will produce a marketable product. For simplicity's sake, assume that the R&D is expected to take three years.

If the research results in what is viewed as a marketable product, the company faces another decision—whether to invest $80 million in the manufacturing and sale of the product. Moreover, uncertainty surrounds the actual success of the product introduction. If the product is successful, the expected cash sales revenues from the product are $200 million each year, compared with an unsuccessful product's revenues of $100 million a year. Furthermore, cash expenses are expected to be 75 percent of sales revenues. The probability of a successful product in this case is 40 percent; the company's marginal tax rate is 40 percent; and the cost of capital is 20 percent, compounded continuously.

Therefore, the Hokie Company has two major decisions to make:
• whether to invest $10 million in R&D, and
• depending on the outcome of the R&D, whether to invest $80 million in the manufacturing and sale of the product, which we shall refer to as production.

This decision process is illustrated in **Figure 2.1**. The Hokie Company's decisions and related probabilities are indicated by boxes; the circles represent outcomes of those decisions.

We shall take a look at how DCF analysis, sensitivity analysis, simulation analysis, decision tree analysis, and option pricing handle this decision process. Because each method uses slightly different information in the valuation, where necessary, we will alter the parameters of the model slightly to help in demonstrating each method.

Traditional Valuation Tools

Capturing the risk in a decision is difficult, but several tools are available that can uncover some of the uncertainty of an investment opportunity. These tools are DCF analysis, sensitivity analysis, simulation analysis, and decision tree analysis.

Discounted Cash Flow Analysis. DCF analysis involves finding a value today—referred to as the net present value (NPV)—of the cash inflows and outflows associated with the investment project. The NPV of a project is the present value of the expected future cash flows discounted at the project's cost of capital less the present value of the project's investment outlays. In the basic form of DCF analysis, the Hokie Company investment presents a challenge because it has two decisions to make—whether to invest $10 million

Figure 2.1. The Hokie Company's Decision Process

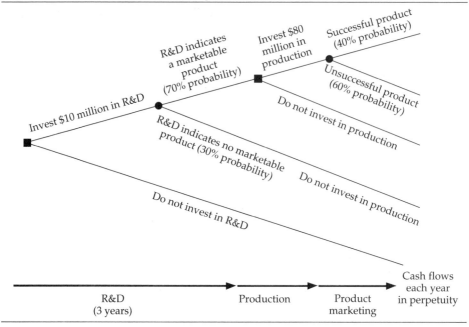

in R&D initially and then whether to invest another $80 million to manufacture and sell the product.

We will start by distinguishing between two NPVs that appear in this problem. At the end of Year 3, conditional on the success of R&D, the company makes a decision whether to invest $80 million in production. This decision at the end of Year 3 is dependent on whether R&D discovers a marketable product. We shall refer to this NPV as the conditional NPV at the end of Year 3, or Conditional NPV_3. The other NPV is the overall project NPV, which is measured as of Year 0, today, the point at which the company must decide whether to invest $10 million in R&D. We refer to this value as the overall NPV, or simply the NPV. Conditional NPV_3 requires several elements:
- the project's useful life,
- the residual or salvage value of the project,
- the expected future cash flows for each period through the end of the project's useful life,
- the amount of the investment outlay, and
- the project's cost of capital.

The useful life is an estimate of the length of time the project is expected to produce cash flows for the company. To simplify the analysis, we assume that the benefits of the project extend indefinitely for the foreseeable future, so we will treat the future cash flows as a perpetuity and not consider a residual value. The expected future cash flows are based on the estimates of the cash flows and their likelihood. The cash flow in the case in which the company chooses to invest in the product is shown in **Table 2.1**.

Table 2.1. Cash Flow for the Hokie Company: Decision to Invest in Product
(millions)

	Successful	Unsuccessful
Cash revenues	$200	$100
Less cash expenses	150	75
Equals cash flow before tax	$ 50	$ 25
Less taxes	20	10
Equals cash flow after tax	$ 30	$ 15

Thus, if the company chooses to invest in the product following R&D, the expected annual cash flow each period, beginning in four years, is as follows:

Expected cash flow = 0.4($30 million) + 0.6($15 million)
= $21 million.

Another element that is necessary to our analysis is the project's cost of capital. The cost of capital is the compensation to suppliers of capital for both the time value of money and risk. This cost of capital should reflect the risk of the project and is often estimated as the cost of capital for the company as a whole or as the cost of capital for projects of similar types. At this point, we shall not get into the details for estimating a project's cost of capital, because such issues are unrelated to the question of how real options enter into investment decisions, but later in this chapter, we show how the volatility of the value of the underlying asset, the project, is related to the cost of capital. In addition, we show how the volatility, value of the asset, and cost of capital interact. For purposes of analyzing this project, we shall just assume that the cost of capital is 20 percent, compounded continuously.[1] If the company

---

[1] With continuous compounding, interest accrues by the factor e^{rT}, where e is the natural log base, 2.71828, r is the continuously compounded rate, and T is the number of years. Suppose interest is paid annually at a rate of 6 percent. After one year, $100 will have grown to a balance of $100(1.06) = $106. The equivalent continuously compounded rate is $\ln(1.06) = 0.0583$, where "ln" indicates the natural log. Then, we can state alternatively that $100 grows by the factor $e^{0.0583(1)}$, which is also 1.06, leading to a balance of $106. An analogous present value factor would be $1/e^{0.0583(T)}$, which is the same as $1/(1.06)^T$.

invests in production of the product, the NPV of this project at the end of the third year (the Conditional NPV$_3$) is as follows:[2]

$$\text{Conditional NPV}_3 = \frac{\$21 \text{ million}}{e^{0.20} - 1} - \$80 \text{ million}$$
$$= \$94.850 \text{ million} - \$80 \text{ million}$$
$$= \$14.850 \text{ million}.$$

Again, the result is the NPV that will be realized at the end of Year 3 if R&D is successful. In some applications, this value is referred to as the terminal value or cash-out price, which is the value at which the project could be sold at that point in time. We focus on the notion that it is a conditional NPV dependent on the success of the R&D. The standard deviation, in millions, is calculated as

$$\text{Standard Deviation} = \sqrt{\left[0.40\left(\frac{\$30}{e^{0.2} - 1} - \$80 - \$14.85\right)^2\right] + \left[0.60\left(\frac{\$15}{e^{0.2} - 1} - \$80 - \$14.85\right)^2\right]}$$
$$= \$33.19.$$

To provide a rough estimate of the implications of these figures, we assume that the distribution of the Conditional NPV$_3$ is normal, meaning that about two-thirds of the time, the Conditional NPV$_3$ would be between plus or minus one standard deviation, which puts the range at –$18.34 million to $48.04 million about two-thirds of the time. Although the Conditional NPV$_3$ is positive, this range is exceptionally large and clearly indicates a significant probability (0.32 assuming a normal distribution) of a negative Conditional NPV$_3$ and thus an undesirable project. Nonetheless, the conditional NPV of the project at the end of the third year is positive when viewed at the decision point of whether to invest in production, so *if* the R&D process generates a marketable product, the investment in the product is expected to add value to the Hokie Company.

Stepping back to the present, we discount this Conditional NPV and incorporate the uncertainty of the R&D to obtain the overall NPV. Thus, an NPV of $14.85 million is realized in three years with 70 percent probability and an NPV of zero dollars is realized in three years with 30 percent probability. The NPV today (in millions) is, therefore,

---

[2]Note that dividing by $e^{0.20} - 1$ reflects the fact that this is a perpetuity.

$$\text{NPV} = -\$10 + (0.70)\left[\frac{\$14.85}{e^{3(0.2)}}\right] + (0.30)(\$0)$$

$$= -\$10 + 5.705 + 0$$

$$= -\$4.295.$$

Thus, after incorporating the uncertainty of R&D and discounting to the present at the cost of capital, the Hokie Company can expect a net loss in value of $4.295 million. This value is the precommitted NPV—that is, the NPV if the Hokie Company makes the decision to definitely invest in production provided that R&D is successful. The Hokie Company might, therefore, be inclined to reject the project. As we will show later, however, the full flexibility available in this project is not being properly valued, which a real options analysis will do.

The DCF analysis allows us to look at only one part of this complex decision process. We have so far ignored a major element of managerial flexibility, which is that the company may or may not invest in production even if R&D finds a marketable product. In addition, the options inherent in a project result in uncertainties that cannot be adequately captured in a single cost of capital, as used in NPV calculations: The risk of the project changes as time progresses, learning takes place, uncertainties resolve themselves, and decisions are made in the future. This is where other approaches can be useful in sorting out these decisions.

Sensitivity Analysis. Estimates of cash flows are based on assumptions about the economy, competitors, consumer tastes and preferences, construction costs, and taxes, among a host of other possible assumptions. One of the first issues we have to consider about our estimates is how sensitive they are to these assumptions. For example, what if revenues in the case of a product with a high potential for success are $140 million instead of $150 million? Or what if Congress increases the tax rates? Will the project still be attractive?

We can analyze the sensitivity of cash flows to changes in the assumptions by re-estimating the cash flows for different scenarios. Sensitivity analysis, also called scenario analysis, is a method of looking at the possible outcomes, given a change in one of the factors in the analysis. Sometimes this analysis is referred to as "what if" analysis—"what if this changes," "what if that changes," and so on. At times a subtle distinction is made between sensitivity analysis and scenario analysis. The former is an attempt to alter input parameters to generate a wide range of possible outcomes. The latter is an attempt to propose a more limited, perhaps very small, number of unusual and oftentimes extreme cases or scenarios. For example, a specific scenario might encompass a worldwide recession coupled with a tax decrease, a Federal

Reserve interest rate cut, and increased volatilities of assets. We will not concern ourselves with these small differences in definitions and will treat the two techniques as the same.

So, we will look at a "what if" for the Hokie Company decision. The sensitivity of the conditional NPV at the end of the R&D period, as of the end of Year 3, for different tax rates is shown in **Table 2.2**. One can see from Table 2.2 that the attractiveness of the project depends on the tax rate; a tax rate of 50 percent instead of 40 percent gives this project a negative conditional NPV at the end of Year 3. If the project is not attractive at the end of Year 3, conditional on R&D success, then it is definitely not attractive at Time 1, because all we do from that point on is multiply by the probability of R&D success, find the present value, and subtract the initial outlay.

As can be seen with this simple example, sensitivity analysis illustrates the effects of changes in assumptions, but because sensitivity analysis focuses only on one change at a time, it is not very realistic. We know that not one but many factors can change throughout the life of the project. We can use our imagination and envision any new product and the attendant uncertainties regarding many factors, including the economy, the company's competitors, and the price and supply of raw material and labor, to name a few.

Simulation. Simulation analysis allows the financial manager to develop a probability distribution of possible outcomes, given a probability distribution

---

Table 2.2. Effects of Changing Tax Rates on Conditional NPV$_3$ for the Hokie Company Decision
(dollars in millions)

Tax Rate	Project Value for a Successful Product	Project Value for an Unsuccessful Product	Conditional NPV$_3$[a]
30%	$[(\$200 - \$150)(1 - 0.3)]/(e^{0.2} - 1)$ = $158.083	$[(\$100 - \$75)(1 - 0.3)]/(e^{0.2} - 1)$ = $79.041	$30.659
40%	$[(\$200 - \$150)(1 - 0.4)]/(e^{0.2} - 1)$ = $135.500	$[(\$100 - \$75)(1 - 0.4)]/(e^{0.2} - 1)$ = $67.750	$14.850
50%	$[(\$200 - \$150)(1 - 0.5)]/(e^{0.2} - 1)$ = $112.916	$[(\$100 - \$75)(1 - 0.5)]/(e^{0.2} - 1)$ = $56.458	-$ 0.958

[a]Conditional NPV$_3$ is the weighted average of the project values for each outcome, where the weights are the probabilities of the outcome occurring minus the outlay of $80.

for each variable that can change.[3] Consider a simplified investment opportunity with only three variables, each of which is uncertain—revenues, costs, and tax rate. We need to specify probability distributions from which random values of these items will be drawn. In this example, we assume that unit sales, price per unit, and expenses are drawn from a normal distribution. We further assume that the tax rate is drawn from a uniform distribution. We have simplified the analysis by assuming that these distributions are independent of one another, but in an actual application, these distributions would not necessarily be independent. For example, unit sales, price per unit, and the tax rates may all be related to the economic environment.

Suppose the following are determined in the case of the Hokie Company:
- Sales are expected to be 10 million units, with a standard deviation of 1,000,000.
- The price per unit is expected to be $14, with a standard deviation of $2.
- The expenses are expected to be 75 percent of dollar sales, with a standard deviation of 5 percent.
- The tax rate falls between 35 percent and 45 percent.

In simulation analysis, a computer program selects random values of input variables and computes an output, which, in this case, would be the project's conditional NPV at the end of Year 3, or Conditional NPV_3. The random outcomes are produced by a routine called a random number generator. Thus, in this example, random values for sales, price per unit, expenses, and the tax rate are selected, which leads to a value for Conditional NPV_3. We now have one outcome. Then we start all over, repeating this process and calculating a new Conditional NPV_3 each time. After a large number of outcomes, we have a frequency distribution, which is a statistical summary of the number of times outcomes are obtained. The outcomes are usually specified in ranges, and the frequency distribution is usually depicted visually in the form of a histogram.

Applying simulation analysis using 1,000 outcomes to the Hokie Company decision produces the distribution of Conditional NPV_3 values shown in **Figure 2.2**. Using standard statistical measures of risk, we can evaluate the risk associated with the return on investments by applying these measures to this frequency distribution. Because the frequency distribution is a sampling distribution (i.e., based on a sample of observations instead of a probability

---

[3]Simulation analysis is widely used in the sciences as well as in operations research. Its origins appear to have been during World War II in the work of the famous mathematician John Von Neumann, who apparently gave it the name Monte Carlo simulation, reflecting the randomness of its approach and the analogy to gambling. It is thought that the first use of simulation analysis in finance was in a capital budgeting application by Hertz (1964). Today, simulation analysis is used extensively in derivatives pricing and risk management problems.

Figure 2.2. Conditional NPV$_3$ Values for the Simulation of the Hokie Company's Project

($ millions)

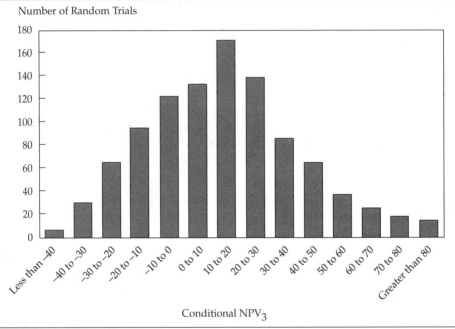

Note: The uncertain factors are sales, price per unit, expenses, and tax rate.

distribution), its standard deviation is calculated in a slightly different manner from the standard deviation of possible outcomes. The standard deviation of a frequency distribution is

$$\text{Standard deviation of frequency distribution} = \sqrt{\frac{\sum_{i=1}^{N}(x_i - \bar{x})^2 f_i}{N-1}},$$

where x_i is the value of a particular outcome, $\bar{x}$ is the average of the outcomes, f_i is the number of times the particular outcome is observed (i.e., its frequency), and N is the number of trials, for example, the number of times a coin is flipped.

The mean of the distribution of Conditional NPV$_3$ values is $13.925 million, and the standard deviation is $26.591 million. The mean is analogous to Conditional NPV$_3$ in the earlier example, and the standard deviation indicates how widely disbursed the simulated Conditional NPV$_3$ values are from this mean. Again, appealing to the normal distribution, we interpret these results as suggesting that the project is expected to add value but that about two-thirds of the time, Conditional NPV_3 will be between –$12.666 million and $40.516 million. In our standard NPV analysis, we obtained a Conditional NPV_3 of $14.85 million and concluded that after accounting for the R&D period, its probability of success, and the R&D outlay, the overall project should not be accepted. So, in this simulation analysis, our mean conditional NPV of $13.925 million would lead to the same conclusion. We might add one further level of analysis, which is that we could simulate the outcome of the R&D process, but without reason to believe that the R&D process is correlated with the costs, revenues, tax rates, and other variables involved in the project, incorporating an R&D simulation would not tell us much more than we already know, which is that its probability of success is 0.7.

Simulation analysis is more realistic than sensitivity analysis because it is capable of introducing uncertainty for many variables in the analysis. But one can easily imagine that this analysis can become quite complex because of the interdependencies among many variables in a given year and the interdependencies among the variables in different time periods. Nonetheless, these interdependencies can usually be incorporated into the analysis, although with a reduction in speed and an increase in complexity.

Simulation analysis, however, looks at a project in isolation, focusing on a single project's total risk. Moreover, simulation analysis ignores the effects of diversification for the owners' personal portfolios. If owners hold diversified portfolios, then their concern is how a project affects their portfolio's risk, not the project's total risk.

Decision Tree Analysis. Decision tree analysis is a method of examining sequential decisions that are subject to uncertainty in the future. A decision tree helps in the analysis of these decisions through the use of a visual roadmap that indicates points of decision and uncertainty. The tree incorporates DCF analysis, providing a basic roadmap of alternative NPVs through the major decisions pertaining to the investment. The base of the tree is the decision made today. That decision can be to make an investment, to decide how much to invest, or to wait. We would like to note, however, that a decision tree is not necessarily much different from a standard NPV analysis. In a standard NPV analysis, the assumption is that any decisions to be made later in a project's life have already been made, whereas a decision tree allows the flexibility to say no to investing any further amount during a project's life. A standard NPV analysis requires that all decisions be made at the start. In a sense, decision tree analysis is like a standard NPV analysis that includes a project review at future decision points.

The decision tree for the Hokie Company's investment dilemma is displayed in **Figure 2.3**. As in Figure 2.1, the Hokie Company's decisions, and related probabilities and payoffs, are indicated by boxes; the circles represent outcomes of those decisions. Although we have arrived at the critical numbers in Figure 2.3 previously, we will review how we got them. Consider the branches in which the Hokie Company invests in the product. The project values for each branch at the end of the third year are as follows:

$$\text{Successful} = \frac{\$30 \text{ million}}{e^{0.20} - 1}$$
$$= \$135.50 \text{ million}$$

and

$$\text{Unsuccessful} = \frac{\$15 \text{ million}}{e^{0.20} - 1}$$
$$= \$67.75 \text{ million.}$$

Figure 2.3. Decision Tree Representation of the Hokie Company's R&D and Production Decisions

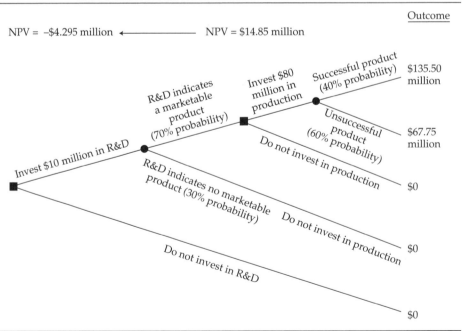

Outcome

NPV = –$4.295 million ←——————— NPV = $14.85 million

Invest $10 million in R&D

R&D indicates a marketable product (70% probability)

Invest $80 million in production

Successful product (40% probability) — $135.50 million

Unsuccessful Product (60% Probability) — $67.75 million

Do not invest in production — $0

R&D indicates no marketable product (30% probability)

Do not invest in production — $0

Do not invest in R&D — $0

As before, the expected payoff of investing in the product, or Conditional NPV_3, is

$$\text{Conditional NPV}_3 = 0.4(\$135.50 \text{ million}) + 0.6(-\$67.75 \text{ million}) - \$80 \text{ million}$$
$$= \$14.85 \text{ million}.$$

As noted previously, the standard deviation of this number is $33.19 million. Basing its decision solely on expected NPV, the Hokie Company would invest if the outcome determined by the R&D process yields a payoff of $14.85 million.

From the decision tree analysis, we know that if the R&D is successful, the Hokie Company will definitely invest in the product. Thus, we would discount this $14.85 million back to the present, weight it by the probability of R&D success, and subtract the initial outlay. Hence, we obtain the overall NPV (in millions) of

$$\text{NPV} = 0.7 \left[\frac{\$14.85}{e^{3(0.20)}} \right] + 0.3(\$0) - \$10$$

$$= -\$4.295,$$

which, of course, is the same value we obtained in the DCF analysis.

Consider the following variation to this problem. Let the outlay required to initiate production at the end of Year 3 be $100 million instead of $80 million. We have already shown that the value of the project to invest at the end of Year 3 is $94.85 million. This value would not change, but the NPV at the end of Year 3 of investing in production would now be –$5.15 million. Consequently, the decision would be made at the end of Year 3 not to invest in production, even if the R&D process produces a successful product. Hence, the value of the project today would obviously be zero and the overall NPV would be –$10 million. The project would be rejected. Because a standard NPV analysis with an outlay at the end of Year 3 of $80 million leads to a negative NPV at Year 0, a standard NPV analysis with an outlay of $100 million at the end of Year 3 would obviously also lead to a negative NPV at Year 0. These two approaches would, in this case, give the same conclusion but with different negative NPVs and for different reasons. Only if the project generates some positive cash flows during the R&D phase would the decision tree approach lead to a different conclusion from the one resulting from the standard NPV approach.

With the flexibility afforded by decision trees, one might expect that we could arrive at the correct value of the project, but such is not the case. Decision tree analysis, like NPV analysis, relies on the use of a single discount rate to value both the project and the option. As we will show later, such an approach is not correct. Decision trees, nonetheless, are useful for mapping out the decision process, especially when there are sequential decisions. As we will show in Chapter 3, a widely used option valuation approach relies heavily on the construction of a tree of sequential outcomes much like a decision tree. In contrast to the decision tree approach, however, option valuation does not require knowledge of the discount rate that reflects risk or knowledge of the actual probabilities of the outcomes. Although option valuation imposes other demands, those demands are far less onerous.[4]

An advantage of using decision tree analysis is its transparency. It does not involve a black box of analytical calculations; it is laid out for all to see. This ability to illustrate the decision points and the uncertainties in a concise, clear form makes decision tree analysis attractive. It is almost surely better than a standard NPV analysis, but neither approach gives the correct answer when real options are involved. To solve that problem, we turn to an approach designed specifically to handle the valuation of options.

Option Valuation

Identifying the options associated with an investment opportunity is the first step toward the correct valuation of real options. The second step is to actually assign a value to these options. Consider an opportunity to defer an investment outlay. This investment opportunity is similar to what a company experiences in its investment in R&D: An expenditure, or series of expenditures, is made in R&D, and then sometime in the future, depending on the results of the R&D, the actions of competitors, and the approval of regulators, the company decides whether to go ahead with the investment opportunity.

In the case of the Hokie Company, it has the decision today, Year 0, to invest in R&D and then a decision at the end of Year 3 to go ahead with production. Consider the elements of the two decisions—the R&D investment and the production investment. If the Hokie Company invests $10 million in R&D, the cash flow today is –$10 million. If the Hokie Company invests in production, the cash outflow is $80 million. But if the Hokie Company makes this production investment, the expected cash flow each year beyond Year 3 is $21 million, as calculated earlier in the DCF analysis. Translating this annual cash flow of $21 million into a project value at the end of Year 3 we arrive at $94.85 million:

$$\text{Project value at Year 3} = \frac{\$21 \text{ million}}{e^{0.20} - 1}$$

$$= \$94.85 \text{ million.}$$

---

[4]See Copeland and Antikarov (2001) for a comparison of decision tree analysis with option valuation.

Subtracting the $80 million investment in production, we find that the conditional NPV at the end of Year 3 is $14.85 million, as shown in **Table 2.3**—a number we have found in previous approaches. As we have already shown, the present value of the cash flows, discounting at a continuously compounded rate of 20 percent and considering the uncertainty of R&D, leads to an expected NPV of –$4.295 million.

Table 2.3. Conditional NPV$_3$ for the Hokie Company Decision
(millions)

	Year 0	Year 3
Investment	–$10.00	–$80.00
Terminal value	0.00	94.85
Net cash flow	–$10.00	$14.85

So, how much is the option to invest in production at the end of Year 3 worth? We shall use the Black–Scholes option-pricing formula to value this option. The Black–Scholes formula for a call option is as follows:

Value of option $= PN(d_1) - Xe^{-rT}N(d_2),$

where

$$d_1 = \frac{\ln(P/X) + [r + (\sigma^2/2)]T}{\sigma\sqrt{T}}$$

$d_2 = d_1 - \sigma\sqrt{T}$

P = the value of the underlying asset today

X = the exercise price

r = the continuously compounded risk-free rate of interest

T = the number of years to expiration of the option

σ^2 = the annualized variance of the continuously compounded return on the underlying asset

$N(d_1)$ and $N(d_2)$ = cumulative normal probabilities[5]

[5] These cumulative normal probabilities are often obtained by looking up values in a table. In this day and age of spreadsheets, one can easily obtain the values through such features as function = NORMSDIST(.) in Microsoft Excel. For example, if d_1 is 1.15, then inserting function = NORMSDIST(1.15) into a cell in Excel gives a value of 0.8749. The interpretation is that the probability is 0.8749 that in a standard normal distribution, which has mean of zero and standard deviation of 1.0, a value of 1.15 or less will occur at random.

Calculating the value of the option requires us to make a couple of assumptions regarding the risk-free rate of interest and the volatility of the project's value. Recall that earlier we assumed a 20 percent cost of capital. Here we will show how we obtained that number. Doing so will enable us to see the important interaction among volatility, project value, and the value of the option. Suppose that the risk-free rate of interest is 4 percent and that the volatility (i.e., the standard deviation of the project's cash flows) is five times the market volatility of 16 percent, or 80 percent. To obtain the cost of capital, we shall need one other piece of information, the risk premium of the market, which we shall take as 3.2 percent. If the volatility is five times that of the market, the risk premium for the project is five times 3.2 percent, or 16 percent. The cost of capital is calculated as the sum of the risk-free rate and the risk premium:[6]

$$
\begin{aligned}
\text{Cost of capital} &= 4 \text{ percent} + 3.2 \text{ percent} \times (80 \text{ percent}/16 \text{ percent}) \\
&= 4 \text{ percent} + 16 \text{ percent} \\
&= 20 \text{ percent.}
\end{aligned}
$$

In the case of the Hokie Company, the current value of the underlying asset is the present value of the conditional value of the project multiplied by the probability that R&D will be successful:[7]

$$
\text{Value of the underlying asset today} = 0.7\left[\frac{\$94.85 \text{ million}}{e^{3(0.2)}}\right]
$$

$$
= \$36.438 \text{ million.}
$$

In other words, the underlying asset, which is the product itself, is currently worth $36.438 million, reflecting its conditional value at the end of Year 3 of $94.85 million times the probability that value can be realized, which is the probability of R&D success. The remaining inputs we require are the exercise price, which is the $80 million investment outlay at the end of the third year, and the number of years to exercise, which is the expected time of the R&D period of three years. Thus, by using the following input values in the Black–Scholes formula—value of underlying asset = $36.438 million; exercise price = $80 million; risk-free rate of interest = 4 percent; volatility = 80 percent;

---

[6]We have used the capital market line, which derives from the capital asset pricing model, to obtain an estimate for the cost of capital. Other methods, however, can be used for estimating a cost of capital.

[7]Technically, we are also multiplying by a conditional NPV at the end of Year 3 of zero dollars for the event that the R&D process does not generate a marketable product times the probability of 0.3 that this outcome occurs.

number of years to exercise = 3—we obtain an option value of $12.744 million.[8] The NPV of the project is the difference between the value of the option and the costs of R&D:

> Project NPV = Present value of R&D costs + Value of the option
> = –$10 million + $12.744 million
> = $2.744 million.

The option value is $12.744 million and costs $10 million. Because this analysis has incorporated all cash flows from the project, as well as the contingency that the $80 million may or may not be invested at the end of Year 3, we have captured the entire financial implications of the project. The project thus has a positive NPV of $2.744 million. Therefore, it should be accepted.

Another way of looking at the contribution of the option to the value of the project is through the concept of strategic NPV versus static NPV. The strategic NPV is the NPV of $2.744 million as obtained above, which incorporates the value of the option. The static NPV is the NPV without the options analysis of –$4.295 million. The value added of the options analysis is the difference between the strategic NPV and the static NPV:

> Value added of the options analysis = Strategic NPV – Static NPV
> = $2.744 million – (–$4.295 million)
> = $7.039 million.

In other words, the options analysis turned a project that appeared to be worth –$4.295 million into one that is worth $2.744 million. This finding does not mean that the option is worth $2.744 million. It means that our static NPV, or traditional DCF analysis, suggested that the project had an NPV of –$4.295 million, whereas the options analysis revealed that the true NPV was $2.744 million. Thus, the options analysis uncovered additional value of $7.039 million.

Note that the option valuation does not indicate whether the company will actually develop the product. Later, if the R&D reveals that the company should not develop the product, it will obviously choose not to do so. Note also that, even if the company develops the product, it may not turn out to be successful. This situation is no different, however, from one in which an investor purchases a call option on a stock, subsequently exercises that option, and then watches the stock perform poorly. The poor performance does not mean that the option should not have been exercised, nor does it mean that

---

[8]Specifically, we obtain (in millions) $d_1 = \{\ln[36.438/80] + [0.04 + (0.80)^2/2]3\}/(0.80\sqrt{3}) = 0.212$, $d_2 = 0.212 - 0.80\sqrt{3} = -1.174$. Then, using Excel, we obtain = NORMSDIST(0.212) = 0.5839 and = NORMSDIST(–1.174) = 0.1202. The option value is, therefore, $36.438(0.5839) - \$80 \times e^{-0.04(3)} \times (0.1202) = \$12.744$. Technically, the answer could vary slightly from the one here depending on the numerical precision of the calculations.

the option should not have been purchased in the first place. The option can be significantly undervalued in the market and well worth purchasing. For the Hokie Company, this option is worth almost 30 percent more than its cost and clearly indicates that the R&D is worth doing.

In the example here, the conditional value of the project at the end of Year 3 was $94.85 million. Because that amount is more than the $80 million investment in production and the probability of R&D success is 0.7, the expectation is that the company will probably invest in production at the end of Year 3. Suppose we alter the terms a little so that the expectation is that the company will not invest in production at the end of Year 3. As we did in the decision tree approach, we will assume that the required investment at the end of Year 3 is not $80 million but $100 million. Now we see that at the end of Year 3, the expectation is still for a conditional project value of $94.85 million, but with the required investment in production of $100 million, we would not expect the company to invest in production. Now we will recalculate the option value today. The value of the underlying asset is still $36.438 million, the exercise price has changed to $100 million, the risk-free rate is still 4 percent, the volatility is still 80 percent, and the number of years is still three. Inserting these values into the Black–Scholes model, we obtain an option value of $10.889 million. This amount exceeds the required initial investment in R&D of $10 million, giving us a strategic NPV of $0.889 million. This value is much smaller than the NPV with an outlay of $80 million but still positive. Recall that a standard NPV analysis, as well as a decision tree approach, the latter of which incorporates a modest degree of flexibility, recommended rejection of the project. But the project adds value, a small amount but value nonetheless. Real options analysis is thus extremely beneficial in identifying those situations in which the outlook for creating value may look deceptively bleak. Standard techniques do not have the flexibility to uncover the hidden values of real options.

Using option pricing in the valuation of a capital project does pose many challenges. One challenge has to do with the parameters in the model. Focusing just on the estimate of volatility, we can see that the value added of the option is sensitive to the estimate of volatility. Although we assumed that the volatility is 80 percent, determining the volatility of a project's future cash flow is not a simple matter. We experience the same problems that we did in trying to determine the beta of a project: It is just not directly measurable. We shall have much more to say about this problem in Chapter 5.

It is well known that in the case of a financial option, a positive relationship exists between volatility and the value of the option. This relationship, however, is static; it holds everything else constant. Economists refer to this type of relationship as comparative statics, which is the analysis of the effect of a change in one input on the output while holding all other inputs constant. For example, suppose we are considering an option on a stock. For whatever reason, the company takes action that increases the risk of the company, which, in turn, increases the volatility of the return on the stock. Holders of call options are quite pleased; their positions increase in value because of the possibility of greater gains.[9] This view, although nearly universally understood in the world of options, is, nonetheless, misleading and can be particularly dangerous when looking at real options. With respect to the option on the stock, if the risk increases but no offsetting increase in the expected return occurs, the shareholders' required rate of return will increase, which will reduce the value of the stock. The lower stock price will then have a negative effect on the price of the option. Whether the increased option value from a higher volatility overcomes the decreased option value from a decrease in the stock price cannot be universally ascertained. So, when someone speaks of an increase in volatility increasing an option's value, it is important to understand that this result is conditional on holding all other effects constant.

In the case of a real option, such a problem might arise if the volatility of cash flows from a project increases. If the value of the underlying asset is not affected by volatility, an unlikely case, a positive relationship would exist between volatility and the value of the option. That is, the greater the volatility, the greater the value of the option. Volatility, however, affects the cost of capital: The greater the cost of capital, the lower the value of the underlying asset. Hence, a greater volatility could have a dampening effect on the value of the option.[10] If the greater volatility reduces the value of the option, volatility could have a negative relationship with the strategic NPV. If we take this last example and calculate the strategic NPV with volatilities of 60 percent and 40 percent, we see that the greater the volatility, the lower the strategic NPV— a result of the effect of an increased cost of capital on the value of the underlying asset on which the option exists. This effect overcomes the beneficial effect of an increase in the volatility on the value of an option, as shown in **Table 2.4**.

Lest we argue that volatility is all bad, note that in the case of volatilities of 80 percent and 90 percent, the value of the option turns what looks like an unattractive project, in terms of the static NPV, into an attractive project. The relationship among volatility, the value of the underlying asset, and the value

---

[9] Option holders benefit from greater potential gains, while not having to worry about greater losses. If the option expires with no value under the original volatility, a higher volatility will not make the loss any worse.

[10] The effect of volatility on the cost of capital, and hence the value of the underlying asset, is often overlooked in simplified demonstrations of real options methodology.

Table 2.4. Hokie Company Investment Project Strategic NPV for Different Estimates of Volatility
(dollars in millions)

	Volatility		
Parameter	70%	80%	90%
Cost of capital[a]	18%	20%	22%
Expected project value, third year[b]	$74.537	$66.395	$59.737
Option parameters			
Value of underlying asset[c]	$43.436	$36.438	$30.875
Exercise price	$80	$80	$80
Risk-free rate of interest	4%	4%	4%
Volatility	70%	80%	90%
Number of periods to exercise	3 years	3 years	3 years
Net present value elements			
Present value of project value	$43.436	$36.438	$30.875
Present value of investment[d]	–32.634	–30.733	–28.944
Present value of R&D costs	–$10.000	–10.000	–10.000
Static NPV	$0.802	–$4.295	–$8.069
Value of the option	14.116	12.744	11.724
R&D expenditure	–10.000	–10.000	–10.000
Strategic NPV[e]	$4.116	$2.744	$1.724

[a]Obtained as risk-free rate + 3.2 percent (volatility/16 percent), where 3.2 percent is the market risk premium and 16 percent is the market volatility.
[b]Obtained as the probability of R&D success multiplied by $21/($e^{\text{cost of capital}} - 1$), where $21 is the expected cash flow.
[c]Obtained as expected project value/$e^{3 \times \text{cost of capital}}$, where 3 is the number of years.
[d]Obtained as $[(0.7)(\$80)]/e^{3 \times \text{cost of capital}}$, where 3 is the number of years, 0.7 is the probability of successful R&D, and $80 is the investment outlay at the end of Year 3.
[e]Obtained from the Black–Scholes model using inputs given above.

added of the option for the Hokie Company's investment are illustrated in **Figure 2.4** for volatilities ranging from 5–100 percent.[11]

Although we have shown how real options valuation can be used to supplement the traditional NPV analysis, there are many complicating issues. For example, most investment projects have several options, some of which interact. If a company is investing in R&D over a period of years in the development of a new product, at least two options exist—the option to abandon during development and the option to defer investment. Because the

[11]Recall that the value of the underlying asset varies with volatility because of the volatility's effect on the cost of capital.

Figure 2.4. Relationship between Volatility and the Strategic Value of the Hokie Company's Project

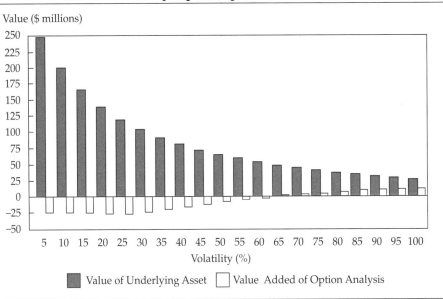

value of one option may affect the value of other options, the valuation problem in the case of multiple options is not simply carried out by adding the separate values. Solving for the value of options in the case of multiple interacting options is beyond the limitations of the Black–Scholes model and is quite difficult, requiring the application of numerical methods.[12]

Summary

Traditional valuation methods, such as DCF, can be modified using sensitivity, simulation, and decision tree analysis to incorporate some managerial flexibility but easily become too complex or unwieldy. Sensitivity analysis provides a way of looking at the effects on a project's value when one factor is allowed to vary, whereas simulation analysis provides a way of looking at valuation with more than one factor varying randomly. Although both methods permit some experimentation with changes in factors, they do not fully capture the flexibility that options inherent in an investment project may offer. And although a decision tree can provide an organized mapping of flexibility options, it uses a single discount rate and fails to capture the true value of these options.

---

[12]For a discussion of these issues and an example of option interactions, see Trigeorgis (1991, 1993a, and 1993b).

Real options valuation offers a method of incorporating managerial flexibility options into the investment decision, highlighting the contributions that these options provide to the investment's strategic value. In the next chapter, we go into more detail on the application of option methods in real options valuation problems and illustrate how the different types of flexibility options can be valued using **binomial trees**.

3. A Framework for the Valuation of Real Options

Determining the value of a real option is not a simple process. Fortunately, a well-developed body of financial theory provides a rich framework from which real options values can be estimated. The theory of option pricing was developed primarily to value financial options, which are options on stocks and stock indexes, bonds, and currencies. To say that it has been successful is perhaps an understatement; the foundations of a multitrillion-dollar global industry are based on the theory of financial option pricing. Every day, large commercial and investment banking firms make markets in financial options for a clientele of corporations, pension funds, and governments.

Financial option-pricing theory does not solve all of the problems of valuing real options, but it does provide a basis for valuing instruments that have similar cash flows and payouts. Note, however, that our use of the term "theory" does not imply an abstraction from reality. Although we shall indeed start with a simple framework, one seemingly far removed from reality, we do so for the purpose of gaining an understanding of the process of option valuation, which is critical to comprehending real options.

Valuation of Financial Options

We begin our investigation of the valuation of financial options by forgetting the world of corporate real assets and focusing on an option on a simple security—an actively traded common stock. Suppose that the stock is priced today at $100. Now we are going to simplify things a little. We shall propose that when the stock price changes during the next period, it can either go up to $150 or down to $50. Thus, the two possible returns on the stock are ($150 − $100)/$100 = 0.50 and ($50 − $100)/$100 = −0.50, or simply +50 percent or −50 percent. We shall use this information in the form of up and down factors u and d, where u = 1.50 and d = 0.50. Thus, u and d are 1.0 plus the return on the stock, or in other words, u and d are holding period returns. For purposes later, we need to introduce the symbols S^+ and S^- to represent the up and down stock prices one period hence (i.e., S^+ = $150 and S^- = $50). Because two outcomes are possible, this approach is typically called the **binomial model** and is often depicted in the form of a binomial tree as shown in **Figure 3.1**. The tree is divided into time points and states. In Figure 3.1, for example, S is

Figure 3.1.   Binomial Tree for a Stock

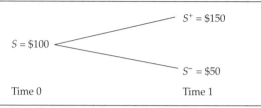

Time 0	Time 1

Notes: S = the value of the stock at Time 0;
S^+ = the value of the stock at Time 1 in the top state; and
$S-$ = the value of the stock at Time 1 in the bottom state.

$100 at Time 0. At Time 1 in the top state, the stock is $150, and in the bottom state, it is $50.

Next we will introduce a call option on the stock. It permits the owner to buy the stock at an exercise price, X. We will set X at $100, the current stock price.[1] One period later, the option expires and permits the holder to buy the stock for $100. Thus, if the stock goes up to $150, the option permits the holder to purchase a $150 stock for $100; at that point, we can say that the option has a value of $50. If the stock goes down to $50, the option permits the holder to buy a $50 stock for $100. At that point, we can say that the option is worthless and the owner will simply let it expire. So, at expiration, given the stock price, we can easily determine the option price. The more difficult task, however, is determining the value of the option today—that is, when the stock is at $100, one period before the option expires.

Because the option's value is determined completely by the value of the stock, it is possible to form an investment that combines the stock and the option to eliminate the risk of losing money. It is also possible to combine a position in the stock and a loan, essentially a risk-free bond, that will precisely reproduce the results that will occur with the option. We shall do just that with our example. But to do so, we shall need one more piece of information, the risk-free rate, r, which we shall let be 5 percent.

Suppose that today we purchase N shares of the stock at $100 and borrow an amount $B. This amount $B is unspecified for right now, but we shall be able to figure it out in a moment. One period later, this combination will be worth $150N - $1.05B if the stock goes to $150 or $50N - $1.05B if the stock goes to $50. Note that the value of the loan is $1.05B, reflecting the fact that

---

[1]There is no reason why the exercise price need be set at the current stock price. Such an option is said to be at the money, which is a common way to structure an option when initiated.

we borrowed $\$B$ and will now owe 1.05 times $\$B$. It turns out that we can force these two investment values to equal the next two values of the option. That is,

$\$150N - \$1.05B = \$50$ if the stock goes to $\$150$ or

$\$50N - \$1.05B = \$0$ if the stock goes to $\$50$.

The above is a set of two equations with two unknowns and has a simple solution:

$N = 0.50$ and $\$B = \$23.81$.

Just as a check on our solution, we can plug in these values for N and $\$B$ and get

$\$150(0.50) - 1.05(\$23.81) = \$50$ and

$\$50(0.50) - 1.05(\$23.81) = \$0$.

What these results mean is that if we purchase one-half of a share of stock and borrow $\$23.81$ at 5 percent, we shall reproduce precisely the results of the call option. In other words, we shall end up with either $\$50$ or $\$0$. If thinking about buying one-half share is bothersome, just scale the problem upwards. For example, multiply everything by 100 to make N equal to 50 shares and the loan ($\$B$) equal to $\$2,381$, which will reproduce the results of 100 call options. We shall continue to just assume one-half share but keep in mind that this amount can be easily adjusted.

Because a combination of purchasing 0.50 shares and borrowing $\$23.81$ reproduces one call option at the expiration of the option, the investment required to establish such a position today must be the same as the value of the call today; that is,

Value of the call $= 0.50(\$100) - \$23.81$

$= \$26.19$.

Because we reproduced the results of the call with 0.50 shares valued at $\$100$ each and a loan of $\$23.81$, we can say this combination replicates the call and is essentially equivalent to a call.

The value of the option, c, can be obtained by a more direct method. We will introduce a simplified variable p given by the formula

$$p = \frac{1 + r - d}{u - d}.$$

This term will be explained later in this chapter. For now we shall just focus on what to do with it. We shall also need p's complement, $1 - p$. The values p and $1 - p$ are then multiplied by the next two possible values of the call, c^+ and c^-, and the result is discounted one period at the risk-free rate. That is,

$$c = \frac{pc^+ + (1-p)c^-}{1+r}.$$

In our example,

$$p = \frac{1.05 - 0.50}{1.5 - 0.5}$$

$$= 0.55,$$

and $1 - p$ is thus 0.45. The option value is, therefore,

$$c = \frac{0.55(\$50) + 0.45(\$0)}{1.05}$$

$$= \$26.19,$$

which is the value we previously obtained. The model is depicted visually in the binomial tree of **Figure 3.2**.

Thus, in the market, the actual option should be selling for $26.19. If the option sells for more than $26.19, someone could sell the option and construct the equivalent position by purchasing 0.50 shares and borrowing $23.81. We call this construction a **synthetic call option**, which is an investment position that replicates the behavior (i.e., the cash flows) of a call option; in this case, the synthetic option consists of holding a long position in the stock and borrowing. The long position in the synthetic option would offset the short position in the actual option so that the overall position would have no risk.

Figure 3.2. Binomial Tree for Stock and Call Option

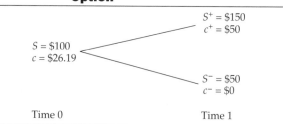

$S = \$100$
$c = \$26.19$

$S^+ = \$150$
$c^+ = \$50$

$S^- = \$50$
$c^- = \$0$

Time 0   Time 1

Notes: See the notes to Figure 3.1 and the following:
  c = the value of the call option at Time 0;
  c^+ = the value of the call option at Time 1 in the top state; and
  c^- = the value of the call option at Time 1 in the bottom state.

If the actual option is selling for more than the synthetic option, it will bring in more money than would be paid out to buy the synthetic option. If the actual option is selling for less than the synthetic option, the synthetic option would be sold. This transaction would be done by selling short one-half share of stock and lending $23.81. The actual option could be bought for less than $26.19. The risks would offset, and yet, a net inflow of funds would occur up front. Either case (i.e., actual option selling for more or less than synthetic option) would be essentially free money. This situation is referred to as an **arbitrage opportunity**.[2]

The combined effects of all investors doing these transactions would force the actual option price to converge to the synthetic option price. Consequently, we conclude that the synthetic option price is the correct value of the option.

The other type of option, a put, gives the right to sell the stock at the exercise price. If this option were a put, the values of the option at expiration would be $0 if the stock was at $150 or $50 if the stock was at $50. That is, the right to sell a $150 stock at $100 is worth zero when it expires, and the right to sell a $50 stock at $100 is worth $50 when it expires. The procedure for the valuation of the put is the same as for the call except that instead of the call values at expiration, the put values are used.

The period of time over which the stock can go from $100 to $150 is the period of time corresponding to a 5 percent interest rate. In other words, $100 invested for one period in a risk-free asset would grow to $105; $100 invested in the stock over this same period would go to either $150 or $50. Suppose the life of the option is two periods and that the interest rate remains at 5 percent for both periods. We shall assume the stock can continue to go up by 50 percent or down by 50 percent. We now have three points in time, which we shall call Time 0, Time 1, and Time 2. The stock prices at Time 2 are denoted as S^{++}, S^{+-}, and S^{--}, corresponding to the stock going up twice, up once and down once, and down twice. The situation is illustrated in **Figure 3.3**.

Now we must recognize that when the option expires at Time 2, the stock will be worth S^{++}($225), S^{+-}($75), or S^{--}($25). So, the three possible option values are

c^{++} = $125 (i.e., the expiring option allows the holder to buy a $225 stock for $100),

c^{+-} = $0 (i.e., the expiring option allows the holder to buy a $75 stock for $100), or

c^{--} = $0 (i.e., the expiring option allows the holder to buy a $25 stock for $100).

---

[2]Arbitrage is the condition that two combinations of instruments provide the same results and yet sell for different values. An arbitrageur buys the cheaper combination and sells the dearer one, thereby eliminating the risk and netting a clean profit of the difference in the prices received and paid.

Figure 3.3. Two-Period Binomial Tree for a Stock

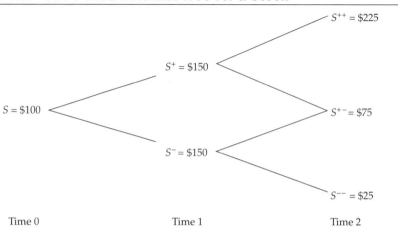

$$S^{++} = \$225$$

$$S^{+} = \$150$$

$$S = \$100$$

$$S^{+-} = \$75$$

$$S^{-} = \$150$$

$$S^{--} = \$25$$

Time 0   Time 1   Time 2

Notes: See the notes to Figure 3.1 and the following:

S^{++} = the value of the stock at Time 2, following an up move at Time 1 and an up move at Time 2;

S^{+-} = the value of the stock at Time 2, following a down move and an up move in Periods 1 and 2, in either order; and

S^{--} = the value of the stock at Time 2, following a down move at Time 1 and a down move at Time 2.

At Time 1, we determine the option values in the same manner that we did in the one-period problem. In fact, at Time 1, we have a one-period problem. The two possible option values at Time 1 are denoted as c^{+} and c^{-}, which correspond to stock prices of S^{+} of \$150 and S^{-} of \$50, and are obtained as follows:

$$c^{+} = \frac{pc^{++} + (1-p)c^{+-}}{1+r}$$

and

$$c^{-} = \frac{pc^{+-} + (1-p)c^{--}}{1+r}.$$

In our problem,

$$c^{+} = \frac{0.55(\$125) + 0.45(\$0)}{1.05}$$

$$= \$65.48$$

and

$$c^- = \frac{0.55(\$0) + 0.45(\$0)}{1.05}$$

$$= \$0.00.$$

Thus, the option value at Time 1 will be either \$65.48 or \$0.00. Note that the second value (c^-) is zero because the option cannot expire with value at Time 2. Next we step back to Time 0 and obtain the value of the option as a discounted weighted average of the values c^+ and c^-:

$$c = \frac{0.55(\$65.48) + 0.45(\$0)}{1.05}$$

$$= \$34.30,$$

which is more than the value of a one-period option, because longer term call options are worth more. The option values corresponding to the stock values for this two-period problem are shown in **Figure 3.4**.

Figure 3.4. Two-Period Binomial Tree for a Stock and Call Option

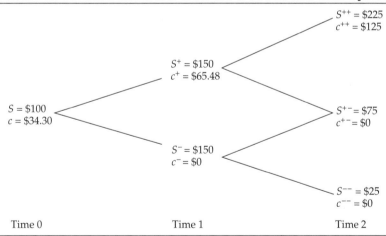

Notes: See the notes to Figures 3.1, 3.2, and 3.3 and the following:

  c^{++} = the value of the call option at Time 2, following an up move at Time 1 and an up move at Time 2,

  c^{+-} = the value of the call option at Time 2, following an up move at Time 1 and a down move at Time 2, in either order, and

  c^{--} = the value of the call option at Time 2, following a down move at Time 1 and a down move at Time 2.

The general procedure for valuing an option in the binomial tree framework, therefore, is as follows:

1. Lay out the binomial tree of stock prices to the period when the option expires.
2. For the period when the option expires, insert the value of the option corresponding to the value of the stock. The value of a call option is the greater of zero or the stock price less the exercise price. The value of a put option is the greater of zero or the exercise price less the stock price.
3. Step back one period prior to expiration. Look ahead at the next two possible option values, multiply them by p and $1 - p$, respectively, add the results, and divide by 1 plus the risk-free rate.
4. Step back one period and repeat Step 3. Continue the process, stepping back one period and repeating Step 3 until Time 0 is reached, at which point the option value is obtained.

Understanding what was done here is not difficult, but accepting that this type of model is realistic may be more difficult. There are, after all, more than two prices to which a stock can move. To make the model more like the real world, we can add a large number of time periods. But if we do so, we may find that having the stock continue to go up or down 50 percent and the interest rate be 5 percent per period is unrealistic. For an option with a fixed life, we can shrink the up and down factors and the risk-free rate so that over the life of the option, the stock price movement and the interest rate are more realistic for that length of time.

We shall not get into the details of this procedure, but one can simply compare this approach with the similarity between taking still photos and making a movie. If we take still photos of a dynamic process, such as a race, we get only a very limited view of what happened. If we take repeated photos at a very rapid rate, we obtain a nearly perfect representation of what happened in the race. Each photo spans a very short time period, but run together, the photos accurately depict reality. Of course, if we have a large number of time periods, we do not want to be calculating the option price by hand, but this process is easily programmable on a computer. For a large number of time periods, the process converges to the well-known Black–Scholes model that we previously mentioned.

For our purposes in this chapter, we shall not need to go into the Black–Scholes model. Our task is not to master the technique of valuing options but, rather, to understand how real world corporate investment decisions give rise to the creation of options that can have significant value. For that purpose in this chapter, we shall continue to use the binomial model. Its simplicity, combined with the knowledge that the model can be extended to a more realistic setting, gives us confidence that it captures the important components of real options valuation.

Valuation of Real Options Using Financial Option-Pricing Models

Real options often arise in corporate investment situations. Consider the scenario depicted in **Figure 3.5**, which is a project of three periods in which the values of the project are given as indicated. The project requires an initial investment of $1,050.

The numbers in the tree represent values of the project. Probably the best way to interpret the project is to assume that at Time 3 the project is terminated and pays the possible cash flows of $3,375, $1,125, $375, or $125. At all previous time points, the numbers represent discounted values of these future cash flows. In other words, the value of the project at a previous period is obtained as the present value of the probability-weighted sum of the next two possible outcomes. Thus, the value of $2,250 at the top state of Time 2 is obtained from the values of $3,375 and $1,125. We will first look at how that value is traditionally obtained.

The company has assessed the risk of the project as requiring a discount rate of 30 percent. To properly value the project, however, we must know the probability of an up and down move. We shall assume the probability of an up move is 80 percent, so the probability of a down move is 20 percent. Now we obtain the value of $2,250 as follows:

$$\text{Valuation of project at Time 2, top state} = \frac{0.80(\$3,375) + 0.20(\$1,125)}{1.30}$$

$$= \$2,250.$$

Figure 3.5. Binomial Tree for a Capital Investment Project

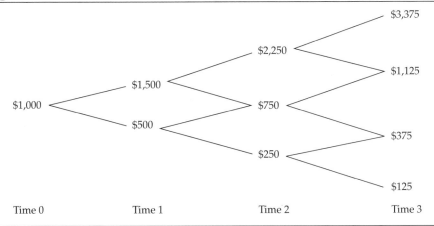

The project is thus worth $2,250 in the top state at Time 2. We can obtain all of the remaining values in the same manner. We see that the value of the project at Time 0 is $1,000, which is obtained as follows:

$$\text{Valuation of the project at Time 0} = \frac{0.80(\$1,500) + 0.20(\$500)}{1.30}$$

$$= \$1,000.$$

With the initial investment being $1,050, the net present value (NPV) of the project is, therefore, –$50. Consequently, the project would be rejected.

Notice that we used the actual probabilities of the two outcomes and the 30 percent discount rate. As it turns out, we can use the same approach to valuing the project as we did in illustrating the valuation of the financial option. For example, to get the $2,250 value we obtained earlier, we can use the weights p and $1 - p$ and discount by the risk-free rate:

$$\text{Valuation of project at Time 2, top state} = \frac{0.55(\$3,375) + 0.45(\$1,125)}{1.05}$$

$$= \$2,250.$$

All of the remaining values can be obtained in a similar manner.

In the first two equations in this section, we used the actual probabilities, weighted the two uncertain outcomes by those probabilities, and discounted at an appropriate rate for the perceived risk. In that sense, the numerator is the expected value of the project in the next period. This expected value is then discounted at the risk-adjusted discount rate. In the third equation, we weighted the outcomes by p and $1 - p$ and discounted at the risk-free rate. Whenever we discount a risky outcome at the risk-free rate, we are assuming that we have either adjusted for risk or that whoever is valuing the project is risk neutral. But it is important to see that the weights p and $1 - p$, which are sometimes called risk neutral probabilities, are not assigned arbitrarily. There is but a single value of p that is consistent with a set of up and down factors and a risk-free rate. Numerous combinations of the actual probability and the risk-adjusted discount rate are consistent with these parameters, but for a given risk-adjusted discount rate, there is but a single consistent value for the actual probability. Alternatively, for a single value of the actual probability, there is but a single consistent risk-adjusted discount rate. The consistency of the risk-adjusted discount rate, the actual probabilities, the up and down factors, the risk-free rate, and the weight p means that either approach works to obtain the value of an asset or option. But when we use the weight p, we do not require the actual probabilities or the risk-adjusted discount rate. In the option-pricing framework, this is the approach normally taken, but it is not required.[3] In the framework in which corporate investment decisions are traditionally analyzed, the former approach (i.e., using the actual probabilities) is normally used.

If the project were as simple as the one depicted in Figure 3.5, the analysis would go no further. But the possibility exists that the project may have one or more real options embedded in it. In such a case, the project could have significant value that is not apparent from a traditional analysis. Many types of real options exist. In some cases, more than one real option exists, and these multiple options can interact, meaning that their values can differ because of the existence of other options. In this monograph, our job is to teach the basics of real options, so we shall keep the examples as simple as possible and allow only one option at a time.

In the analysis that follows, we take a close look at three options—the **growth option**, the **deferral option**, and the **abandonment option**. A number of other types of real options exist. Appendix A contains an overview of several of these options, with illustrations in the binomial model context used in this chapter. Appendix B presents an adaptation of the binomial valuation approach used in this chapter to the Hokie Company example in Chapter 2.

Growth Option. One of the most common types of options is a growth option, sometimes called an **expansion option**. When a company has a growth option, it has the opportunity at a date later during the life of the project to invest additional funds and expand the project's scale. Suppose that at Time 1 in the example illustrated in Figure 3.5 the company has the opportunity to invest an additional $900 and expand the size of the project by 70 percent. Thus, if it invests the additional $900 at Time 1, all values at Times 2 and 3 will be larger by a factor of 70 percent. **Figure 3.6** shows the binomial tree under the assumption that the project is expanded at Time 1. Note that the figure does not show a value at Time 0 because that value is meaningless. The numbers in the figure show values under the condition that the project is expanded, but this figure does not reflect the exercise of the option to expand. As shall be seen, in one situation the company will decide to exercise the option and in another it shall decide not to exercise it. After we have accounted for the option, we can properly obtain the value of the project at Time 0.

These values in Figure 3.6 are obtained as follows. At Time 3, the previously determined values shown in Figure 3.5 are all increased by a factor of 1.70:

$3,375 \times 1.70 = \$5,737.50$;
$1,125 \times 1.70 = \$1,912.50$;
$375 \times 1.70 \quad = \$637.50$;
$125 \times 1.70 \quad = \$212.50$.

---

[3] We shall have a lot more to say about this point in Chapter 5.

Figure 3.6. Binomial Tree for a Capital Investment Project with Expansion Undertaken at Time 1

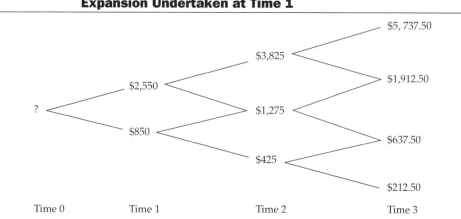

| Time 0 | Time 1 | Time 2 | Time 3 |

The values at Time 2 can be calculated based on the new Time 3 values. For example,

$$\frac{[0.8(\$5,737.50) + 0.2(\$1,912.50)]}{1.30} = \$3,825.$$

But they can also be obtained by the same procedure used to get the Time 3 values (i.e., multiplying the results in Figure 3.5 by 1.70):

$2,250 × 1.70 = $3,825;
$750 × 1.70 = $1,275;
$250 × 1.70 = $425.

The values of the project at Time 1 are obtained in a similar manner:

$1,500 × 1.70 = $2,550;
$500 × 1.70 = $850.

The company must invest the additional $900 at Time 1 to get these values. In the top state at Time 1 with the new investment, the value of the project is $2,550, but when we subtract the additional $900 invested, we get a market value of $1,650. In the bottom state, the project is worth only $850 if the $900 is invested, so the company will not exercise the growth option. Now we need a new binomial tree. This one is a bit more complex and is illustrated in **Figure 3.7**.

Note that this tree in Figure 3.7 is somewhat different from the other ones in this chapter. Observe the addition of two outcomes at Time 3. In Figures 3.5 and 3.6, the tree had four unique outcomes at Time 3, but there were actually eight outcomes: up-up-up, up-up-down, up-down-up, down-up-up, down-down-up, down-up-down, up-down-down, and down-down-down. Until

Figure 3.7. Binomial Tree for a Capital Investment Project with a Growth Option

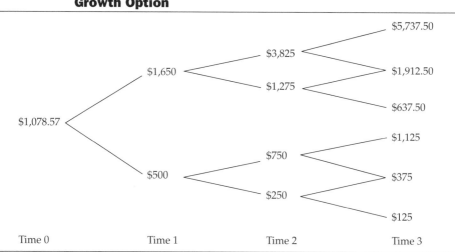

| Time 0 | Time 1 | Time 2 | Time 3 |

now, two ups and one down led to three identical end results, as did two downs and one up. But with the exercise of the growth option at Time 1, an up move at Time 1 is followed by values that are 70 percent higher. A down move at Time 1 is followed by values that are the same as the ones without the growth option. The result is that the tree now has six outcomes at Time 3. In other words, the exercise of the option in the top state at Time 1 means that a move of up-down-down is not the same as any other combination of two downs and one up. In addition, down-up-up is different from an up followed by either down-up or up-down.

Determining the market value of the transaction is also now more complex. We cannot simply use the actual probabilities and the 30 percent discount rate. The new project is different from the original project. Consequently, the risk is different, so a new risky discount rate is required. As a result, we do not know the true discount rate. Option-pricing theory, however, assures us that we can value the project using the risk neutral probabilities. We did, after all, value the original project using risk neutral probabilities and obtained the correct value of $1,000 and an NPV of –$50. By using **risk neutral valuation**, we do not have to concern ourselves with the risk or appropriate discount rate.

Thus, we can obtain the values at Time 1 by using risk neutral valuation in the following manner:

$$\text{Value of the project in the top state at Time 1} = \frac{0.55(\$3,825) + 0.45(\$1,275)}{1.05}$$

$$= \$2,550$$

and

$$\text{Value of the project in the bottom state at Time 1} = \frac{0.55(\$750) + 0.45(\$250)}{1.05}$$

$$= \$500.$$

Because the company chose to invest $900 in the top state at Time 1, the value will have to be adjusted to $2,550 – $900 = $1,650. The company shall not invest in the bottom state; hence, the outcomes are the same as if the growth option did not exist.

We can now step back to Time 0 and obtain the overall project value as follows:

$$\text{Value of the project at Time 0} = \frac{0.55(\$1,650) + 0.45(\$500)}{1.05}$$

$$= \$1,078.57.$$

Subtracting the initial outlay of $1,050 from the project value, we obtain a new NPV of $28.57. Because the overall project was worth –$50 without the growth option and $28.57 with the growth option, the growth option is worth $28.57 – (–$50) = $78.57.

Note that we can value the option separately if we can identify the payoffs upon exercise of the option, which is easy to do in this case. At Time 1, exercise of the growth option in the top state increases the value of the project from $1,500 (shown in Figure 3.5) to $2,550 (shown in Figure 3.6), a gain of $1,050. In the bottom state, it increases the value of the project from $500 (shown in Figure 3.5) to $850 (shown in Figure 3.6), a gain of $350. Thus, the two outcomes of the one-period option are $1,050 and $350. The exercise price is $900. The option values at expiration are, therefore, $1,050 – $900 = $150 and $0, the latter result occurring because the company would not pay $900 more to obtain a gain in value of only $350. Thus, the option value today is

$$\text{Value of the option at Time 0} = \frac{0.55(\$150) + 0.45(\$0)}{1.05}$$

$$= \$78.57,$$

which is the value previously obtained.

Although all of the real options illustrated here can be analyzed and valued in the context of the option alone (as we just showed), normally the valuation is easier if the option is not separated from the remainder of the project and the entire project is simply valued with the option included. Then, the option value can be ascertained by subtracting the NPV of the project without the option, which is the approach we shall follow from here on out.

The existence of the option to expand turned the project from an unacceptable one to an acceptable one. An analogous example in the real world is a company investing in a project that is unattractive without the expansion option. Once the project has started, this company can learn valuable lessons about the demand for its products and whether its infrastructure will support expansion into other and related products. That type of situation occurred in the example in this section. Think of the top state at Time 1 as representing an early favorable outcome for the project. If it occurs, the company invests more funds and expands the project. If an unfavorable outcome occurs, the company does not expand.

Deferral Option. Many projects do not require that the company initiate the project today. That is, either the initial investment is made today and the project begins generating value or the initial investment is deferred until a later date and, if done at that time, the project begins to generate value from that point on. Although many projects require that the company move quickly, considerable value can be gained by waiting to resolve some of the uncertainty. Although waiting can permit competitors to gain an advantage, it can reveal valuable information about the nature of the market. One need look no further than the fact that Microsoft did not develop the first or even second spreadsheet, word processor, or presentation software.

Suppose we consider once again the capital investment project diagrammed in Figure 3.5 and introduce an option to defer the initial investment. Specifically, assume that the company has the opportunity to make the initial outlay ($1,050) at Time 1 instead of at Time 0 with the stipulation that the initial investment required will be higher than $1,050 if the company waits until Time 1. Thus, we will have to factor in a reasonable increase in the required initial investment. Because our purpose is illustrative, we shall simply use the risk-free rate; it should be obvious that we could adjust for a higher rate. So, if the company invests at Time 1, it must invest

$1,050 \times 1.05 = $1,102.50.$

For the decision of whether to invest at Time 1, note that the value of the project is $1,500 in the top state and $500 in the bottom state (as shown in Figure 3.5). Thus, the company should be willing to invest in the former state and not in the latter. Consequently, we can think of this problem as being an option with an exercise price of $1,102.50, where the value of the underlying will be either $1,500 or $500. If the value turns out to be $1,500, the company will make the investment and receive a value of $1,500 − $1,102.50 = $397.50. If the value turns out to be $500, the company will not invest. Thus, we must replace the value of $500 with $0 because the project will not have any further value. As previously done, we obtain the value of the project at Time 0 as follows:

$$\text{Value of the project at Time 0} = \frac{0.55(\$397.50) + 0.45(\$0)}{1.05}$$

$$= \$208.21.$$

Because the project had an NPV of –$50 without the deferral option and $208.21 with the deferral option, the option value is $208.21 – (–$50) = $258.21. We illustrate this problem in **Figure 3.8**.

Figure 3.8. Binomial Tree for a Capital Investment Project with a Deferral Option

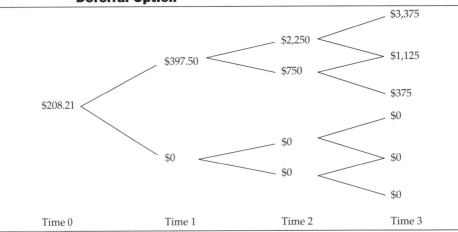

Time 0	Time 1	Time 2	Time 3

$208.21 → $397.50 → $2,250 → $3,375 / $1,125
$750 → $1,125 / $375
$0 → $0 → $0 / $0
$0 / $0

If the company had an option to invest even later, this option could possibly have even greater value. In this case, it would be a call option with a longer time to expiration, which is always worth more. If, however, the increase in initial outlay required were higher than the risk-free rate, any benefits of waiting could be overcome by the increased outlay.

Abandonment Option. During the life of a project, a company can choose to terminate the project by investing nothing further in it. This choice is called the **option to default**. Some default options are accompanied by the opportunity to obtain a salvage value from the project. This type of option is typically called the abandonment option. We will take a look at the more general option to default in Appendix A.

To understand the abandonment option and the role of salvage value, we need to go back to the original project, illustrated in Figure 3.5, in which $1,050 is invested today. Assume that at Time 1 the company can terminate the project and receive a value of $700, which is simply like selling off the project to someone else. In the top state at Time 1, the project has a value of $1,500, so the company has no reason to abandon it. In the bottom state at Time 1, the project has a value of $500. In that case, terminating the project and receiving $700 would be worthwhile.[4] Thus, the value of the project at Time 0 with this abandonment option is

$$\text{Value of the project at Time } 0 = \frac{0.55(\$1,500) + 0.45(\$700)}{1.05}$$

$$= \$1,085.71.$$

With the initial outlay of $1,050, the NPV is $35.71. The option added $35.71 − (−$50) = $85.71 in value. The project is illustrated in **Figure 3.9**.

Figure 3.9. Binomial Tree for a Capital Investment Project with an Abandonment Option

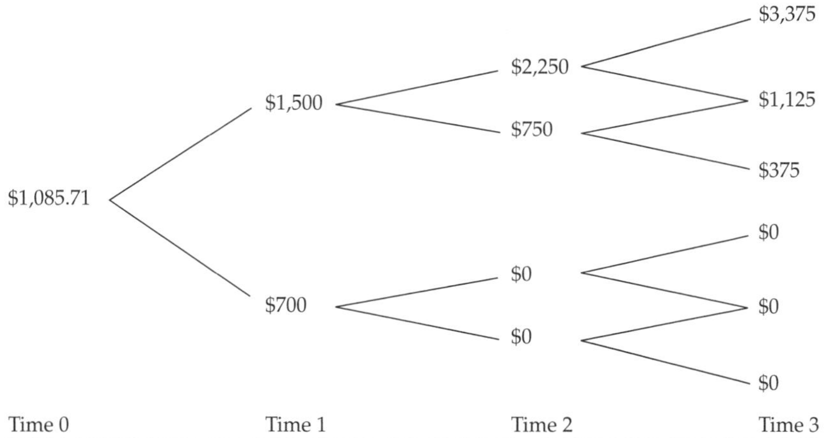

Summary
=======

The valuation of real options in practice is never quite as simple as what we have done in this chapter. We do not live in a three-period world in which project values can move to only two possible new values. But extending the analytical methodology to enable us to value options in a world of multiple times and outcomes is not too difficult. Although the valuation technology has a solid foundation, structuring an actual real options problem is not always simple and straightforward. What we have shown in this chapter is not how to handle every situation in the real world but how to establish an understanding of *why* real options add value. We now move on to more realistic applications of real options models in the next chapter.

---

[4]One might reasonably inquire as to why another company would offer $700 for a project worth only $500. The answer lies in the fact that the other company may have synergies in its existing business that enable it to use the assets of this project more productively than the original company.

4. Getting Real about Real Options

Real options valuation has been suggested as a way of helping investors determine whether a company's stock is over- or undervalued. Traditional valuation metrics, such as P/E multiples, do not explain the valuations of many companies that are believed to have substantial real options. For example, even ignoring obvious differences caused by risk, valuing an online retailer using multiples created to evaluate "bricks-and-mortar" retailers may not fully capture the effect of the new technology and the exploitation of new markets. As we discussed in Chapter 1, the difference between the value based on traditional techniques and that observed in the market can be substantial, which is not to say that all such differences are explained by options. Rather, for some companies, real options can explain at least part of this difference. In this chapter, we shall look at some of these concerns more closely by examining several real-world examples. In addition, we will construct a hypothetical case study, using a step-by-step cookbook approach to the valuation of a company with real options.

Applying Real Options Valuation

A recent article in the *Financial Analysts Journal* illustrates nicely the nature of the problem of valuing a company with real options and how that valuation can differ significantly from the market's valuation. Kellogg and Charnes (2000) analyzed the value of a biotechnology company, Agouron Pharmaceuticals, using decision tree and binomial tree approaches. Biotech companies are well known for having high values during periods when their products are in the lengthy development phase—when the products are not generating any positive cash flows. Clearly, such companies possess a number of real options of the type we have previously covered. For example, these companies can terminate a project if they believe that it will not increase shareholder wealth or can possibly expand the project if market conditions are more favorable than they anticipated.

Kellogg and Charnes found that valuations of Agouron based on real options differed from the actual market values of the company's stock as a particular drug progressed through the development process. We summarize their findings with the graph in **Figure 4.1**. Note the increasing spread

Figure 4.1. Actual, Decision Tree, and Binomial Model Valuations of Agouron Pharmaceuticals' Stock Price, June 30, 1994, to December 23, 1996

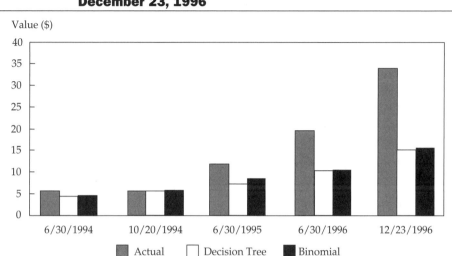

Source: Based on Table 4 in Kellogg and Charnes.

between the market's valuation and the valuations obtained using the binomial and decision tree methods. Kellogg and Charnes attributed the increasing deviation between the real options valuation and the stock's actual value to different assumptions used by their models and shareholders. For example, investors evidently assumed that a particular drug would take eight years to reach the market, when, in fact, it took less than two. Different assumptions about the probability distribution of sales also accounted for some of the difference. The important point in this case is not that real options were overlooked by the market but, rather, that they may actually have been overvalued by the market.

In the same issue of the *Financial Analysts Journal*, Schwartz and Moon (2000) examined the valuation of Amazon.com stock to determine the level of volatility and company profitability that would explain the current value of the stock. They found that the value of the stock could be explained only if expected volatility were almost twice the historical volatility or if profitability in the future were five times reasonable expectations based on Amazon's current and historical revenues and expenses. Although Schwartz and Moon did not attribute this discrepancy specifically to real options, real options are apparently responsible for a significant amount of the difference. For example, Mauboussin (1999) specifically identified the following real options of Amazon:

- **scope-up options**—opportunities to enter into different product lines,

- **scale-up options**—opportunities to expand capacity,
- **learning options**—opportunities to acquire companies and enter into joint ventures that give Amazon the ability to enter into new businesses that it has little experience with, perhaps using what it learned in these ventures to help its existing product lines, and
- equity stakes—ownership of interests in related start-up ventures, or in other words, equity interests in real options owned by other companies.

Indeed Amazon's viability in light of its poor profitability and cash flow is undoubtedly a result of its ability to develop and optimally exercise its real options; however, analysts and investors do not have an easy time recognizing and properly valuing a company's real options. Failure to recognize real options can lead to a market price that greatly understates the true value of a company. Likewise, real options can also be overvalued. Misvaluation of real options is, in all likelihood, a result of not knowing how to properly value real options, not using reasonable inputs, or not considering the interaction of the many real options a company possesses.

We will next take a look at an actual company that unquestionably holds many real options to determine the difference, if any, between the market's valuation and a valuation based on traditional discounted cash flow (DCF) methods.

Valuation of Cisco Systems

To see how real options can make valuing a company difficult, consider the valuation of Cisco Systems, a well-known supplier of networking products. Our valuation task is facilitated somewhat by the fact that Cisco has no long-term debt and does not pay dividends. The market value of equity of Cisco Systems on August 10, 2000, the day following the release of its fiscal year 2000 (FY2000) earnings information, was $445.1 billion. How much of this value is based on the options that Cisco has and how much is based on the present value of future cash flows from its assets in place cannot be easily determined. Nonetheless, we will investigate the valuation of Cisco first using traditional metrics and then looking at the difference between actual market value and the value determined by these traditional metrics. This difference in valuation we believe can be attributed at least in part to Cisco's real options.

A DCF valuation requires that we make forecasts of future cash flows, estimate the company's cost of capital, and then discount those cash flows at the cost of capital. Along the way we will have to make a host of assumptions. This analysis is not intended to provide a precise value of the real options embedded in Cisco's stock price. Indeed, we are not privy to the details of the real options that Cisco holds. We provide this analysis simply as a guide to an approximate value of these real options as well as a means for facilitating an understanding of the role of real options in traditional investment analysis.

The forecasted earnings of Cisco for the next year (i.e., FY2001) are $0.72 per share, or $5.0544 billion, and for the following year, they are $0.95 per share, or $6.669 billion.[1] Although forecasts for the years beyond two years into the future are not specifically available, we can use the forecasted growth rate to project earnings three to five years into the future. A forecasted growth rate of 31.3 percent gives the future earnings per share (EPS) and net income for Cisco shown in **Table 4.1**.[2]

Table 4.1. EPS and Net Income for Cisco Based on a Growth Rate of 31.3 Percent

Year	EPS	Net Income (billions)
2001	$0.720	$ 5.054
2002	0.945	6.669
2003	1.241	8.775
2004	1.630	11.513
2005	2.140	15.093

Because we are interested in valuing future cash flows, we need to estimate cash flow by making an adjustment to earnings for capital expenditures and depreciation. Cisco's capital expenditures tended to exceed depreciation by approximately $100 million in each of the past three years (1997, 1998, and 1999). Thus, a reasonable adjustment to earnings to arrive at cash flows seems to be to subtract $100 million, producing the cash flow numbers shown in **Table 4.2**. Of course, we also require earnings beyond the next five years. Traditional techniques usually require one to assume that at some point in time in the future, earnings begin to grow at a constant long-term rate. We will assume that Cisco's earnings will grow at a 10 percent rate beyond 2005. We also need to specify the cost of capital for Cisco. Using *Value Line Investment Survey*'s estimate of Cisco's beta of 1.45 and assuming a risk-free

[1]Yahoo! Finance is used as the source of forecasted earnings, forecasted growth rates, market capitalization, and price multiples. *Value Line Investment Survey* is used for all other financial data.

[2]These projections were based on FY2000 results and projections made at the end of FY2000. As with most forecasts, the actual results differ from the projections. In the case of Cisco in FY2001, it had a significant loss resulting from restructuring charges and from the impairment of inventory.

Table 4.2. Net Income and Cash Flow for Cisco
(billions)

Year	Net Income	Cash Flow
2001	$ 5.054	$ 4.954
2002	6.669	6.569
2003	8.775	8.675
2004	11.513	11.413
2005	15.093	14.993

rate of 5 percent and a market risk premium of 6 percent, Cisco's cost of capital is estimated to be 13.7 percent. In addition, we need to make an assumption regarding capital expenditures and depreciation. If we assume that growth in earnings will slow beyond five years, we can reasonably assume that capital expenditures will approximate depreciation, so no adjustment needs to be made to earnings to arrive at cash flow.

The terminal value of Cisco, using a constant growth model, is as follows:

$$\text{Terminal value}_{2005} = \frac{\$15.096 \text{ billion } (1.10)}{(0.137 - 0.10)}$$

$$= \$448.800 \text{ billion.}$$

The discounted value of Cisco's future cash flows (in billions) is, therefore,

$$\text{DCF} = \frac{\$4.954}{1.137} + \frac{\$6.569}{(1.137)^2} + \frac{\$8.675}{(1.137)^3} + \frac{\$11.413}{(1.137)^4} + \frac{\$14.993 + \$448.800}{(1.137)^5}$$

$$= \$266.565.$$

Comparing this value with the current market value of $445.100 billion produces a difference of $178.535 billion. Of course, some of that difference could be simply misvaluation by the market or misspecification of the parameters in the valuation just given. If we vary the parameters slightly, we can see that the difference between market value and DCF value is highly dependent on these parameters. For example, if we assume that the growth rate beyond 2005 is 11 percent instead of 10 percent, all other things being equal, the difference between market value and cash flow value is only $91.061 million. Or, if we assume that the required rate of return is 16 percent instead of 13.7 percent, the difference between market value and cash flow value is $284.873 million. We can even vary the parameters to give a negative difference between market value and cash flow value. Clearly, all of this difference cannot be option value. For some companies, perhaps little, if any, of this difference is option value. Thus, this quantitative analysis must be supplemented with a qualitative analysis of the reasons why a company might or might not have real options.

Cisco is such a large and widely followed company that it is unlikely the market is overvaluing it by 67 percent. In addition, based on the analysis of Mauboussin, we have good reason to believe that Cisco has a large number of real options, such as the following:

- scale-up options: Cisco is the leader in supplying networking equipment for Internet connectivity and thus has great potential to expand its capacity.
- scope-up options: Cisco is positioned to offer the broadest array of Internet connectivity products, which allows it to expand into any of these product areas as consumers and businesses demand.
- learning options: Recent acquisitions have resulted in Cisco obtaining key technology, such as the ability to integrate voice, video, and data in a single network.

Some of this apparent overvaluation is likely caused by Cisco's real options. If we attribute all of the difference between market value and DCF value to real options, we can also approximate the option value using multiples. Using the P/E multiple, we see that Cisco's current P/E is 117.9. The average P/E for the S&P 500 is 25.2. If we apply the S&P 500's multiple to Cisco's earnings, we arrive at a value for Cisco of $95.1 billion. If the difference between the current valuation and that estimated from applying the S&P 500 multiple is attributed to the value of Cisco's real options, then the options are valued at $350 billion, a value much higher than the one found using DCFs. We do not know, however, how much of the difference is caused by real options, but we have good reason to believe that some of it is.

Case Study in Valuing a Company with Real Options

A comprehensive valuation that includes all the types of real options would be quite complex and is beyond the scope of this monograph. We can, however, get an idea of how to apply option pricing to the valuation of a company using a simplified example with one option.[3] In this example, we put ourselves in the position of a financial analyst and illustrate the step-by-step procedure that an analyst would follow in valuing a company with real options.

Step 1. Gather the Information. Consider the discounted valuation of a hypothetical start-up company, the Nole Company, whose forecasted cash

---

[3]This example is modeled after the approach used by Luehrman (1998a). For an example of valuing a start-up venture, see Amran and Kulatilaka (1999a, 1999b) and Kulatilaka (1999).

flows for six years are provided in **Table 4.3**. These cash flows are calculated using a number of assumptions:

- The initial start-up costs consist of $500 million of capital expenditures and $50 million of investment in working capital. Without considering any expansion, depreciation and capital expenditures are each $100 million a year.
- At the end of three years, the company has the opportunity to expand by investing $2 billion. This expansion will result in additional annual depreciation of $200 million a year, although no additional annual capital expenditures are needed after this expansion. That is, annual capital expenditures will be $100 million a year in Years 4 through 6.
- Revenues are forecast for each of the next six years as $1 billion for Year 1, $1.2 billion for Year 2, $1.44 billion for Year 3, $1.9 billion for Year 4, $2.47 billion for Year 5, and $3.211 billion for Year 6. These revenues include the opportunity to expand. If the company does not expand, revenues are expected to be $1 billion in Year 1, $1.2 billion in Year 2, $1.44 billion in Year 3, $1.526 billion in Year 4, $1.617 billion in Year 5, and $1.715 billion in Year 6.

Table 4.3. Valuation of the Nole Company with the Expansion Option
(millions)

		Year					
	0	1	2	3	4	5	6
Revenues		$1,000	$1,200	$1,440	$1,900	$2,470	$3,211
Less: cost of goods sold		700	840	1,008	1,330	1,729	2,248
Gross profit		$ 300	$ 360	$ 432	$ 570	$ 741	$ 963
Less: selling and general expenses		50	60	72	95	124	161
Operating profit		$ 250	$ 300	$ 360	$ 475	$ 618	$ 803
Less: taxes		88	105	126	166	216	$ 281
Earnings after taxes		$ 163	$ 195	$ 234	$ 309	$ 401	$ 522
Add: depreciation		100	100	100	300	300	300
Less: capital expenditures	$500	100	100	2,100	100	100	100
Less: change in working capital	50	0	0	300	0	0	0
Cash flow	−$550	$ 163	$ 195	−$2,066	$ 509	$ 601	$ 722
Terminal value[a]							$4,634
Present value of cash flow	−$550	$ 133	$ 131	−$1,134	$ 229	$ 221	$ 217
Present value of terminal value							$1,396
Net present value	$643						

[a]Terminal value = $750/e^{0.20 - 0.05} - 1 = $4,634.

- Cost of goods sold is 70 percent of revenues.
- Sales and general expenses are 5 percent of revenues.
- The tax rate is 35 percent.
- The cost of capital is 20 percent, compounded continuously.
- Cash flow for Year 7 is assumed to be $750 million if the company decides to expand but only $290 if it does not expand. The growth rate of cash flows beyond Year 6 is assumed to be 4 percent a year.

Step 2. Value the Company without Considering the Option. The valuation shown in Table 4.3 indicates a DCF value of $643 million. By not considering the flexibility offered by the expansion option, however, DCF valuation does not give an accurate picture of the full value of the company. The analysis in Table 4.3 simply assumes that the expansion will definitely be undertaken.

As a first look at the problem, suppose we determine the value of the company without the expansion. Then we can compare the value with the expansion with the value without the expansion. In this way, we can determine an upper and lower bound on the value of the expansion option.

The cash flows and valuation of the company without the expansion are shown in **Table 4.4**. Without the expansion, the value of the company ($674 million) is higher than with the expansion ($643 million), suggesting that the expansion would not add value. The separate DCF value of the expansion option itself is shown in **Table 4.5**, indicating that the expansion reduces the value of the company by $31 million. At this point, we might conclude that the expansion has negative value and that the Nole Company would choose not to exercise that option, thereby making the option have zero value. As we will show next, however, this conclusion is wrong.

Step 3. Value the Option. The DCF valuation ignores the flexibility of the option to expand or not. This flexibility can have a remarkably large value, because conditions can change between today and three years from now. The Nole Company should not make a decision today on whether to exercise an option that does not expire for three years. We will now look at the value of the expansion option using more appropriate methods. We first need to specify the parameters of the option. These parameters are shown in the top of **Table 4.6**. The exercise price is the value of the outlays, $2 billion in capital expenditures plus an increase in working capital of $300 million for a total of $2.3 billion. The value of the underlying asset is the present value of the cash flows from the expansion (as found in Table 4.5), or (in millions) $117 + $125 + $133 + $856 = $1,231. The life of the option is three years because the expansion decision takes place at the end of the third year. The risk-free interest rate is assumed to be 6 percent.

Table 4.4. Valuation of the Nole Company without the Expansion Option
(millions)

				Year			
	0	1	2	3	4	5	6
Revenues		$1,000	$1,200	$1,440	$1,526	$1,617	$1,715
Less: cost of goods sold		700	840	1,008	1,068	1,132	1,210
Gross profit		$ 300	$ 360	$ 432	$ 458	$ 485	$ 515
Less: selling and general expenses		50	60	72	76	81	86
Operating profit		$ 250	$ 300	$ 360	$ 382	$ 404	$ 429
Less: taxes		88	105	126	134	141	150
Earnings after taxes		$ 163	$ 195	$ 234	$ 248	$ 263	$ 279
Add: depreciation		100	100	100	100	100	100
Less: capital expenditures	$500	100	100	100	100	100	100
Less: change in working capital	50	0	0	0	0	0	0
Cash flow	−$550	$ 163	$ 195	$ 234	$ 248	$ 263	$ 279
Terminal value[a]							$1,792
Present value of cash flow	−$550	$ 133	$ 131	$ 128	$ 111	$ 979	$84
Present value of terminal value							$504
Discounted cash flow	$674						

[a]Terminal value = $290/e^{0.20 - 0.05} - 1 = \$1,792$.

As noted previously, volatility is a critical variable in the analysis of option values. By definition, volatility is the standard deviation of the continuously compounded return on the underlying asset. In this case, the expansion and its ensuing cash flows are treated as an underlying asset with a value that fluctuates from year to year. We estimated the current value of this underlying asset at $1.231 billion. While making that estimate, we need to derive an estimate of the volatility of that number. We must keep in mind that we need to convert the year-to-year relative values to continuously compounded returns before we can estimate the standard deviation of that series. As an example, the current value is estimated at $1.231 billion. Suppose the following year's value is $1.348 billion. The relative return would then be $1.348 billion/ $1.231 billion = 1.0951. The continuously compounded return is thus ln(1.0951) = 0.0908, or 9.08 percent. The standard deviation of year-to-year continuously compounded returns is the volatility. We should keep in mind that the number we obtain for the volatility must be consistent with assumptions from normal probability theory. That is, for example, a volatility of 0.5 means that the continuously compounded returns vary around their average

Table 4.5. Valuation of the Nole Company's Expansion Option
    (millions)

	\multicolumn{7}{c}{Year}						
	0	1	2	3	4	5	6
Revenues					$374	$853	$1,496
Less: cost of goods sold					262	597	1,047
Gross profit					$112	$256	$ 449
Less: selling and general expenses					19	43	75
Operating profit					$ 94	$213	$ 374
Less: taxes					33	75	131
Earnings after taxes					$ 61	$139	$ 243
Add: depreciation					200	200	200
Less: capital expenditures				$2,000	0	0	0
Less: change in working capital				300	0	0	0
Cash flow				$2,300	$261	$339	$ 443
Terminal value[a]							$2,842
Present value of cash flow				−$1,262	$117	$125	$ 133
Present value of terminal value							$ 856
Discounted cash flow	−$31						

[a]Terminal value = $460/e^{0.20 - 0.05} - 1 = $2,842$.

such that about two-thirds are within ±50 percent (one standard deviation) and 95 percent are within ±100 percent (two standard deviations). Suppose that for similar projects we observe the distribution shown in **Figure 4.2**. This distribution has a mean annual return of 35 percent and a standard deviation of 50 percent. Thus, our volatility estimate is 50 percent.[4]

Using the Black–Scholes option-pricing model, as we illustrated in Chapter 2, the value of this option is $245 million, as shown in Table 4.6. This analysis results in a total value of the company, considering the value of the expansion option, of $919 million. Thus, the option has significant value compared with our previous analysis, where it appeared to have no value. Moreover, in our DCF analysis, we concluded that the option was not worth exercising. Under the option-pricing methodology, the company does not decide today whether the option, which expires in three years, should be

---

[4]Clearly, we are not dealing with a truly normal distribution; we shall assume it is close enough for illustrative purposes.

Table 4.6. Calculating the Nole Company's Strategic Value
(millions)

Black–Scholes parameters	
Value of underlying asset	$1,231
Exercise price	$2,300
Number of periods	3
Volatility	50%
Risk-free rate	6%
Black–Scholes elements	
d_1	–0.0809
d_2	–0.9469
$N(d_1)$	0.4678
$N(d_2)$	0.1718
Strategic value of the Nole Company	
Value of expansion option	$ 245
Discounted cash flow value of the Nole Company without the option	674
Strategic value	$ 919

Figure 4.2. Distribution of Annual Returns

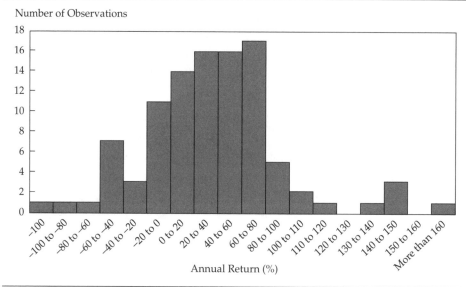

Note: This distribution has a mean of 35 percent and a standard deviation of 50 percent.

exercised. Indeed, the company shall simply wait three years and then the decision will be clear cut. The value of waiting is, therefore, substantial.[5]

Step 4. Examine Sensitivities. In spite of our best efforts, the estimated value of the option could be wrong. Among other things, we may have the volatility wrong. When the volatility alone is changed, the value of any option changes by a significant amount and in the same direction as the volatility change. In the case of a real option, however, changing the volatility also changes the cost of capital. Thus, if the volatility increases, the cost of capital increases, which lowers the value of the underlying. This change, in turn, lowers the value of the option, thereby offsetting some or all of the benefit of greater volatility. As one may recall, we discussed this point in Chapter 2. The effect of different volatilities is shown in **Figure 4.3**. We see an inverse relationship, which is counterintuitive to what option-pricing theory tells us. But again, two effects need to be considered, not just one. Regardless of the sensitivity of the option value to the volatility, the option definitely has value.

The traditional DCF approach indicated that the option had no value and should not be exercised. But, in fact, it is nearly impossible for an option-valuation analysis to give a zero value for an option today. A zero value could be obtained only in some unusual cases, such as the underlying asset having zero current value or its value being below the exercise price combined with zero volatility. An exercise price of infinity can also produce an option value of zero. And, of course, an option value of zero could be obtained if the option is expiring immediately and the underlying asset value is worth less than the exercise price. Thus, other than these very unusual circumstances, an option's value today will always be nonzero, contrary to what a DCF analysis might reveal.

Some Final Comments. If we had not used option-pricing methods and simply had proceeded until Year 3, the possibility exists that if conditions had changed, the company, using traditional DCF methods, might still have chosen to exercise the expansion option and ultimately added value from the expansion. The problem with that way of thinking is that it implies that today the company is incorrectly valued. Its option to expand is assumed to be worth nothing, and the market grossly undervalues the company. For the company

---

[5]A similar situation is described by Shapiro (1993). In his discussion of the problems with capital budgeting methods, he points out that a negative net present value project may provide a valuable option if it provides, for example, a foothold in a market. Such a project may provide the company with the option to expand in that market at a later date, yet traditional DCF methods would not have considered this option to wait to be valuable.

Figure 4.3. Value of the Expansion Option and the Static Value of the Nole Company for Different Levels of Volatility

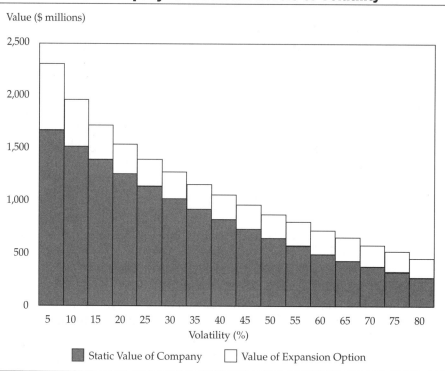

itself, this error is simply one of a market failing to recognize value when it exists, but for financial analysts, this error is especially critical because they are failing to recognize valuable wealth-creating opportunities.

Summary

In this chapter, we examined several practical applications of real options. Admittedly we are unable to consider all of the complexities of the real world in our illustrations. But this is where financial analysts earn their keep. The use of professional judgment and years of experience, combined with an understanding of real options, enables the analyst to obtain more accurate fair values of the companies under consideration.

Before moving forward, let us review what we have done so far. In Chapter 1, we discussed the evolution of real options in financial decision making and how option-pricing methods can be applied to investment opportunities in real assets. In Chapter 2, we described the valuation methods used traditionally in capital budgeting and showed how real options valuation can supplement DCF analysis to capture the strategic value of an investment. In Chapter 3, we illustrated, using binominal trees, the different types of real options and their valuations. In the present chapter, we applied real options to the valuation of a company that had an expansion option.

Up to this point, we have presented real options valuation as it has been written about in the academic and practitioner literature. A remarkable observation from reading this literature is that real options valuation may seem to be the cure for all valuation problems. Virtually all examples are presented as though one can easily recognize real options, obtain input values, and apply real options analysis without concern as to whether mistakes are being made or whether using real options analysis is even appropriate. In short, there is a dearth of criticism on the limitations and difficulties of using real options valuation. Thus, in the following chapter, we will take a more critical look at this methodology.

5. Pitfalls and Pratfalls in Real Options Valuation

In the previous chapters, we examined the many attractions of using real options valuation for corporations and especially financial analysts. One might get the impression that real options valuation is easy to do or that it is an infallible financial tool. Indeed, a reading of the literature on the subject reveals a notable absence of criticisms and limitations. But, in fact, real options valuation suffers from numerous criticisms and limitations and can be particularly difficult to implement. Some of these criticisms are relatively minor, but some are quite important.[1] In this chapter, we attempt to address some of the concerns associated with real options valuation, noting weaknesses along with strengths, identifying criticisms that are valid and those that are not, and showing a more balanced view than is generally found elsewhere. We stress that our goal in this monograph is neither to glorify real options valuation nor to tear it down. Our goal is to inform. To that end, we argue that real options valuation is a powerful tool, but as with all powerful tools, it must be used properly with a recognition of its limitations and weaknesses.

We also would like to emphasize that our treatment of these issues is at a basic level. Our objective is a modest one—to apprise the reader of issues, concerns, and caveats. We do not have the space to devote to providing a detailed explanation or resolution of these issues. Indeed, many of the issues are open to considerable debate among the most knowledgeable scholars and practitioners and are unlikely to be resolved in the near future.

Complications from Internal and External Interactions

As we illustrated extensively in Chapter 3 and Appendix A, the body of knowledge of financial option-pricing theory forms the basis for understanding real options valuation. Unfortunately, real options valuation suffers from a few subtle problems that often are missing from situations involving financial options. For example, consider the case of a typical financial option in which an investor buys an option on Microsoft stock (MSFT). The option's value is based on its potential payoffs, which are determined by the performance of MSFT. With the possible exception of the investor being Bill Gates or another

---

[1]For an excellent treatment of some myths associated with real options, see Mayor (2001).

senior officer at Microsoft, an investor cannot influence the performance of MSFT. When real options are involved, however, the holders and writers of these options (the investors) are generally the companies whose performance *is* the underlying asset. Obviously, a company can influence the value of its stock. Thus, in the case of real options, the option holder would be able to influence the value of the underlying asset. This possibility violates the assumptions on which option-pricing models are based.

Consider a simple real option in which a company can abandon a project and receive a salvage value if it so desires. We illustrated a project of this type in Chapter 3. The company can increase the value of this option by engaging in actions that increase the volatility of the underlying asset's value. Such actions permit the company to potentially gain on the upside if the option is not needed and yet not lose more on the downside if the outcome is bad. But further complicating this matter is the fact that if the company increases the volatility of the underlying asset's value, the value of the underlying asset might decrease. It would make good economic sense for the company to take actions that set the volatility of the underlying to the level that maximizes the overall value of the project plus the option. In the absence of the option, the company might not attempt to raise the volatility of the value of the underlying asset. Option-pricing models, however, require that the underlying be valued separately without the effects of the option. This value and volatility then enter exogenously into the valuation of the option.

Thus, interactions between the option holder and the underlying asset's value can complicate the analysis of real options. But is this problem unique to real options? No, even some financial options are subject to this concern. For example, when a company issues a convertible bond, it effectively sells a call option on the stock to the bondholders. The bondholders do not influence the value of the underlying asset, but the company, which is the option writer, obviously influences this value. The company could engage in actions that lower the volatility of the value of the underlying asset for the purpose of making the option less valuable. In a similar manner, a company issues warrants on its own stock. So, again, the company also affects the value of the underlying asset. Thus, the writer of the option can exert influence on the underlying asset.

Lest one think that only writers of financial options can influence the underlying, consider the case of executive stock options. These options are held by executives, who clearly can influence the performance of the underlying asset.

In addition to the potential for the option holder to influence the underlying asset's value, real options are complicated by the possibility of competitor reactions that might influence the underlying asset. Consider the abandonment option just described. Suppose a company exercises its option to abandon a project. That decision may appear to be optimal in isolation: The salvage value exceeds the market value of the project. But suppose the company abandons the project and then competitors, smelling an opportunity, step up their efforts to service the company's customers, potentially siphoning away business from another part of the company. For that reason, many companies are known to engage in low-profit or even loss-leading activities because of fear that competitors will take customers away, which would result in the loss of other revenues. Thus, the company might even exercise an out-of-the-money option or fail to exercise an expiring in-the-money option. In highly competitive environments, real options are extremely complex because of this added element of the uncertainty of competitors' reactions. And because competitor reactions are decisions made by humans, they too are subject to a great deal of uncertainty. Competitors may react or may not, even when it might appear rational to do otherwise.

These points can be summarized by saying that most financial options adhere to the rule that the value of the underlying asset is in no way influenced by whether the option is exercised. In real options, no such rule exists.

Inability to Explain Absurd Valuations

Consider again the abandonment option, specifically the example in Chapter 3. In that example, the project without the option to abandon is worth $1,000 (as shown in Figure 3.5). With the option to abandon, the project is worth $1,085.71 (as shown in Figure 3.9). Thus, the option is worth $85.71. The project itself is worth almost 12 times the value of the option. In fact, for most options, the underlying asset is usually worth many times the value of the option. For call options, the value of the underlying asset is the upper limit on the value of the option. For puts, the exercise price (assuming an American option) is the upper limit on the value of the option.[2]

These points should immediately call into question the notion that a real option can make a company be worth many times its fundamental value.[3] Certainly, a company that has one real option probably has other real options. The collective values of these options can add up to a significant amount, but it is unlikely that a company is so blessed with real options that an overall value of many multiples of its fundamental value is obtained. Moreover, when a

---

[2]For European options, the delay involved in waiting to exercise the option at expiration means that the upper limit of the option value is the present value of the exercise price.

[3]A more rigorous explanation with an example of this point is provided in Mayor.

company has multiple real options, those real options are usually not independent of each other. Thus, their values are not strictly additive. Therefore, it is extremely questionable whether the presence of real options can explain the seemingly absurd prices that were witnessed in recent years for many Internet stocks. Real options undoubtedly account for some, but certainly not all, of these value differentials.

Model Risk

Model risk is defined as the risk associated with the use of an incorrect model or incorrect inputs in an otherwise correct model or the incorrect use of a correct model, which includes such problems as programming errors and mistakes in entering otherwise correct inputs. The following provides a quick overview of the potential dangers of model risk for standard options. Consider an American put option on a stock priced at $100. The exercise price is $100, the risk-free rate is 5 percent, the time to expiration is one year, and the volatility is 32 percent. The correct model, a binomial model that adjusts for early exercise, gives the value as $16.41. If a European model, such as Black–Scholes, is used, the price will be $15.48, an error of $0.93, or 5.7 percent. If the correct model is used but the volatility is slightly misestimated at 30 percent, the value will be found to be $15.64, an error of $0.77, or nearly 4.7 percent. If the correct volatility of 32 percent is transposed and entered incorrectly as 23 percent, the option price is $13.01, an error of $3.40, or almost 21 percent. And if the formula is programmed incorrectly, anything is possible. Although model risk can create large errors, even small and subtle errors can add up.

Model risk has emerged as an area of concern to specialists in options.[4] Model risk is much less severe for simple European-style financial options than for American-style options. The input parameters are somewhat easier to identify, and the general consensus is that the Black–Scholes model is appropriate for the type of option in question. Model risk usually becomes a greater concern as the option becomes more complex. And as we have noted many times, real options tend to be fairly complex. So, for real options, a much greater danger exists that one will use the wrong model or bad inputs in the right model. How much skepticism this danger should raise in one's mind before using real options is difficult to judge. If nothing else, it should force one to think long and hard about getting the right model, the right inputs into the model, and making no mistakes at the implementation stage.

---

[4]See the excellent treatment of model risk in Figlewski (1998).

Failure to Meet Assumptions

A model should not be judged by whether the assumptions on which it is based are realistic. Model builders make assumptions for the purpose of simplifying reality in the hope that the essential characteristics of a complex process can be captured and incorporated into a framework that leads to realistic explanations and/or predictions of results. Hence, a model is a good model not because it meets assumptions but because it explains reality. The old adage of not throwing the baby out with the bathwater applies as much to model building as it does to anything else.

Nonetheless, in some cases, reality departs so significantly from the assumptions of a model that before using the model, one begins to question its appropriateness. Nowhere is this caution more critical than in real options valuation. Whether a model works well is usually determined by examining the results of empirical studies. Unfortunately, real options valuation does not lend itself easily to empirical validation. Although a few tests have been made of real options models, and we shall examine these later in Chapter 6, accepting the validity of real options models relies heavily on one's faith in the models. Hence, the validity of the assumptions is more important than might be the case for many other financial models for which the abundance of statistical data makes empirical testing much easier.

We will examine the assumptions of real options models by classifying them into major assumptions and minor assumptions. The former are assumptions that are critical. The latter are commonly made assumptions but ones that can be relaxed, albeit with more complexity that may not always be worthwhile.

Major Assumptions. The major assumptions of real options valuation are **lognormality**, randomness, and known and constant volatility over time.

■ *Lognormality.* One of the foremost assumptions in option-pricing models is that the rate of return on the underlying asset is lognormally distributed. When dealing with an option on a stock, the rate of return would be defined as the percentage change in price plus the dividend yield, if any. If the rate of return is lognormally distributed, then the logarithmic return is normally distributed. For example, if a nondividend-paying stock sells for $100 and then moves up to $110 over the course of one year, the return is 10 percent. The logarithmic return is $\ln(1.10) = 0.0953$, or 9.53 percent. That is, the $100 stock growing at 9.53 percent continuously will attain a value of $110 in one year (i.e., $100e^{0.0953(1)} = 110$).[5] The continuously compounded return is the logarithmic return. Option-pricing models typically assume that the

---

[5]See also Footnote 1 in Chapter 2.

logarithmic return follows a normal distribution, which means that the return itself (i.e., without taking the logarithm) follows a lognormal distribution.

The lognormal distribution is a particularly appealing one in financial models based on stock returns. A normal distribution permits unlimited losses, but a lognormal distribution truncates losses on the downside, which is consistent with the fact that shareholders have limited liability. Moreover, the general consensus is that the lognormal distribution provides a better fit to actual data, given that it also possesses positive skewness.

Most of the mathematical models of option pricing are based on the notion of a lognormal distribution. It may appear that the binomial model does not assume a lognormal distribution, and that assumption is true for the simple cases used in this monograph, but in practice, binomial trees should be much larger than the ones we have illustrated. When expanding the tree, certain formulas tell the user what numbers to place in the tree for the underlying asset values. These formulas are based on the assumption of a lognormal distribution.

The assumption of lognormality is controversial for many types of options. For example, most experts agree that the prices of energy products do not follow the lognormal assumption, but options on these products are often priced using the lognormality assumption. Bond and interest rate options are often priced based on lognormality, even though the assumption probably does not hold. In addition, many people do not believe that stock returns are lognormally distributed, and some empirical evidence suggests that this belief may be the case.[6] More importantly, however, for our purpose is whether the values of assets underlying real options follow lognormality. They almost surely do not, but this conclusion does not mean that we should reject the model. Others have not done so with other option-pricing problems, as described earlier, because the alternatives are no better and potentially are worse. The advantages gained from the assumption of lognormality are often considered well worth the deviation from reality for most applications. And in some cases, departures from lognormality can be appropriately taken.[7]

Is the assumption of lognormality a likely problem for real options valuation? The values of underlying real assets almost surely exhibit properties

[6]For example, the existence of multiple implied volatilities for a single stock, based on options with different exercise prices but the same expiration, a phenomenon called the volatility smile, is suggestive of violations of the lognormality assumption.

[7]For example, managers of financial asset portfolios are often concerned with the likelihood of large losses. These "tail events" are almost universally believed to occur with greater frequency than that suggested by a lognormal distribution. Thus, when focusing on tail events, such as in value-at-risk calculations or stress tests, departures from lognormality are appropriate.

that make them behave differently from those of financial assets. For example, real assets do not trade in an open, liquid, and very efficient market. Whether those differences violate the assumption of lognormality sufficiently to warrant a rejection of real options models is difficult to tell. But those differences do give cause for concern and force users of real options models to proceed with some caution.

■ *Randomness.* Virtually all models for pricing financial instruments are based on the notion that prices evolve randomly. Randomness is a necessary component of financial models, because it assures that markets are competitive and that no one participant or group of participants dominates all others. In financial terminology, markets are required to be efficient, or at least sufficiently efficient, to assure the competitiveness that allows pricing models to work.

Options on financial assets are generally considered to comply with this requirement. The markets for stocks, bonds, and currencies are relatively, and perhaps highly, efficient. But the markets for the assets that underlie real options are not necessarily efficient. These underlying assets represent projects, products, and capital investments and, accordingly, are known as real asset markets. Real asset markets are definitely not efficient. The existence of positive net present values (NPVs) that companies pursue and sometimes generate in their goal of maximizing shareholder wealth is evidence of this fact. Companies, particularly new ones, operate in highly inefficient markets, exploiting new ideas and technologies to produce positive NPVs, also known as economic profits. The underlying asset is, therefore, an instrument that does not trade in an efficient market. But the models for pricing real options are based on the assumption that the underlying trades in an efficient market. Whether this problem is sufficiently important to invalidate real options models is not clear, but it is a concern that one must keep in mind.

■ *Known and constant volatility.* Although some advanced option-pricing models incorporate changing volatility, the assumption that the volatility is known and does not change through time is a common and critical one. Option-pricing models are notoriously sensitive to the volatility. Moreover, the volatility is the only variable in standard option-pricing models that is not directly observable and relatively easy to obtain. Recall that option-pricing models require the exercise price, the time to expiration, the price of the underlying, the risk-free interest rate, and the volatility. The first two items are written into the option contract; the price of the underlying is generally observable in the market; and the risk-free rate can usually be obtained from the rates on risk-free assets in the market. The volatility, however, is not directly observable and must be estimated. To make matters worse, volatility is itself notoriously volatile. A market may be more or less volatile today than it was yesterday. The notion of a volatility of volatility gives rise to a host of problems that have stumped even the experts on financial option pricing.

So, even though option-pricing models tend to require known and constant volatility, in reality, the volatility is neither known nor constant. The consequences of this problem are likely to be quite severe. Although the sensitivity of option prices to volatility is probably no more acute in the real options arena than in the financial options arena, the estimation of volatility for real options is a greater concern. Because of the special difficulties of estimating volatility for real options, we will address the topic of volatility estimation later in this chapter.

Minor Assumptions. The minor assumptions of real options valuation are a known and constant risk-free rate, no taxes and transactions costs, no cash flows on the underlying, and use of European-style options. These assumptions are somewhat less critical than ones we just described.

▪ *Known and constant risk-free rate.* Option-pricing models generally assume a known and constant risk-free rate. Although some controversy surrounds which interest rate is the best proxy for the risk-free rate, some comfort can be taken in knowing that most option-pricing models are not very sensitive to the risk-free rate. The rate on a Treasury bill maturing at the option expiration is the most often used proxy for the risk-free rate, but others argue that a rate more reflective of a high-quality private borrower is more appropriate. Nonetheless, values obtained using option-pricing models, with the exception of those in which the underlying is a bond or interest rate, are not very sensitive to the risk-free rate, so reasonable errors can be tolerated.[8]

▪ *No taxes and transaction costs.* Financial models nearly always assume the absence of taxes and transaction costs. Such simplifications facilitate the capture of the most essential elements of the economic process being modeled. As it turns out, real options models may suffer less from this problem than financial option-pricing models do. The market value of the underlying asset is normally obtained through standard discounted cash flow (DCF) analysis, which nearly always incorporates taxes and all costs associated with owning the asset. Furthermore, any other costs connected with the ownership of real options either are captured in the model or can usually be added. Any taxes can, and should, be incorporated into the cash flows and market values in a real options model. So, if taxes and transaction costs are ignored, the fault lies not with the real options valuation process but, rather, with the user.

▪ *No cash flows on the underlying asset.* Standard binomial and Black–Scholes models of option pricing are typically derived for the case of an option

---

[8]See pp. 178–179 in Chance (2001).

on an individual stock. In the simplest case, the stock pays no dividends. Consequently, there are no cash flows on the underlying asset. And if the stock pays dividends, incorporating them into the analysis is not difficult, although several methods can be used and it is not always clear which approach is the best.

In the case of real options, however, cash flows on the underlying asset are an essential component of the analysis. The underlying is typically a project, which generates cash inflows and outflows. As illustrated in previous chapters, these cash flows affect the value of the real option, and they most definitely are incorporated into the analysis.

■ *European-style options.* A European-style option is one that can be exercised only at expiration. An American-style option is one that can be exercised any time prior to expiration and is best handled using binomial trees. Because of the tremendous flexibility they offer, real options are often of the American style. Hence, binomial trees are commonly used in valuing real options. Although binomial trees add some complexity and increase the computational demands, they afford the flexibility required by most real options problems.[9]

Difficulty of Estimating Inputs

One of the major criticisms of real options valuation is that estimating the inputs required in the model is difficult. As it turns out, however, the necessary information is no more demanding than for a simple DCF/NPV analysis of the underlying project itself. In fact, the demands are far less. We shall return to this point later in this section, but for now, we will examine the information required for real options analysis.

As we discussed earlier, to value an option, the user must know the market value of the underlying, the exercise price of the option, the risk-free rate, the time to expiration, and the volatility of the underlying. Each of these inputs is discussed below.

Market Value of the Underlying Asset. The market value of the underlying is the value of the project that the real asset is based on. Normally, this value is estimated based on a DCF analysis. Although estimating the DCF value of such a project is not easy, the analysis is no more difficult when real options are involved. Companies routinely perform NPV analyses. Even though estimating the appropriate discount rate, the life of a project, and all of the cash

---

[9]Although closed-form solutions, such as the Black–Scholes model, are used when possible, binomial trees are clearly the preferred approach in the three major books on real options: Amran and Kulatilaka (1999b), Trigeorgis (1996), and Copeland and Antikarov (2001).

flows may be difficult, those problems existed well before anyone recognized the existence of real options, and they exist even when real options are absent. Our goal in this monograph is not to address all of the problems associated with valuing capital investment projects in the absence of real options. We believe *if it is not possible to value the project without any options attached to it, then the project itself should not be considered. If the project should not be considered, then any real options associated with it should not be considered.*

Nonetheless, a few technical considerations must be understood when determining the value of the underlying project. Interestingly, the literature on real options has overlooked this problem. We will identify and discuss this problem here, but we cannot resolve the issue.

Consider the example of a deferral option from Chapter 3. In the basic example (shown in Figure 3.5), the underlying project is worth either $1,500 or $500 at Time 1, and the project is worth $1,000 today, Time 0. The initial outlay is $1,050, so the NPV is –$50; thus, the project by itself would not be accepted. But the company has an option to defer the investment one year, as shown in Figure 3.8. At that time, the company could invest the greater amount of $1,102.50 ($1,000 adjusted for the risk-free rate) and start the project then. In that case, the value of the project at Time 0 is $208.21. Thus, the option turned an NPV of –$50 to an NPV of $208.21, so the option to defer is worth $258.21.

What is the market value of the underlying project? It is not the NPV of –$50 but, rather, the value of the project in the market (i.e., its cost) of $1,050. That is, investing in the underlying project would cost $1,050. The NPV reflects a decision to purchase the underlying project and gives the economic value if the investment in the underlying is made. If the underlying is a stock whose value is $1,000 but costs $1,050 in the market, the value of $1,050 would be used in the real options valuation process. The market is assumed to know the true value of the underlying. Even if that value is not correct, real options models (indeed *all* option-pricing models) are based on the understanding that the underlying asset can be purchased and used in a hedge with the option. Even if that idea is untenable, and we will discuss this point in detail later in this chapter, one must acknowledge that the true purchase price of the underlying project is whatever the market demands.

Strangely, however, the literature on real options consistently treats $1,000, the calculated value of the project, as the value of the underlying asset, even though one could not enter into the project for that price. The inconsistency arises from the fact that option-pricing theory, on which real options valuation is based, is grounded in the assumption that the assessed market value of the underlying is the value it would sell for in the market. In other words, we are back to the notion that the market is efficient. Option-pricing models make no attempt to inject into the model inefficiency in the market for the underlying. Indeed, there is no way to do so. And even though only two pieces of information are needed about the underlying to value the real option based on the underlying—its market value and its volatility—real options theory is based on the notion that one must value the underlying, often requiring one to perform an NPV analysis and usually finding a nonzero NPV. Most real options models take the assessed market value of the underlying as an input. This input is then used as the underlying asset price in a Black–Scholes-type analysis or as the initial value in a binomial tree from which future values are calculated.

We shall not attempt to resolve this issue here, but we present it to demonstrate that the state of real options theory is such that it has not recognized all of its problems.

Exercise Price. The exercise price in a real options analysis is the amount that would be paid or would be received if a real option is exercised. For example, in the option to abandon, the project is terminated early if the amount that can be received for terminating the project is more than the market value of the project. But the amount that can be received for a project at a future date is potentially quite difficult to determine. Consider a plant that a company might want to abandon. It would have to determine the exercise price based on its assessment of the potential future market value of the plant. Such a situation gives rise to the notion that the exercise price, as well as the market value of the underlying, could be a variable itself. Although the handling of such a situation is complex, option-pricing theory does include models that can accommodate such cases.[10]

In the example in the previous section of the deferral option, a similar problem could exist. The company could choose to defer the investment for a year, or perhaps later in other situations. The company would then have to estimate how much more it would have to invest if it deferred the outlay. In the problem we worked in Chapter 3, we assumed that the required outlay grows at the risk-free rate. Obviously, we could assume any other rate, but the possibility always exists that we do not know at what rate the initial investment will increase.

We cannot go through all the types of real options and the different problems one might encounter in identifying the exercise price. Suffice it to say that one needs to either know the exercise price for certain, have a very

---

[10]The exchange option model of Margrabe (1978) is suited quite well for this scenario.

reliable estimate of it and an acceptance of the consequences of error in that estimate, or be prepared to use more sophisticated models.

Risk-Free Rate. Fortunately, real options valuation escapes serious problems when it comes to the risk-free rate: One simply needs to know the opportunity cost of money. Although some minor issues are discussed in the literature from time to time, generally it is acceptable to obtain an estimate of the risk-free rate by estimating the rate on a default-free zero-coupon security. For example, consider a situation in which a real option expires in 275 days. Let the bid and ask discount rates on U.S. government zero-coupon bonds (Treasury bills) for that maturity be 4.52 percent and 4.54 percent, respectively. One generally splits the difference and assumes a rate of 4.53 percent. The price of a one-year T-bill is

$$\text{Price} = \text{Face value} - \text{Discount rate} \left(\frac{\text{Days to maturity}}{360} \right)$$

$$= \$100 - 4.53 \left(\frac{275}{360} \right)$$

$$= \$96.54.$$

Although getting an exact match between the option maturity and the real options expiration may not always be possible, one should come as close as possible or interpolate between adjacent rates. Note that the denominator of 360 days is always used to find the price in the U.S. T-bill market.

If the T-bill price is \$96.54 per \$100 par, the annual rate is

$$\text{Rate} = \left(\frac{\text{Face value}}{\text{Price}} \right)^{(\text{Days to maturity}/365)} - 1$$

$$= \left(\frac{100}{96.54} \right)^{365/275} - 1$$

$$= 0.0478.$$

Note that in annualizing, 365 days is used. The exponent is the number of 275-day periods in one year.

The rate of 4.78 percent would be appropriate for the binomial model. To use the rate in a model such as the Black–Scholes model, one would need to obtain its continuously compounded analog, which would be

$$\ln(1.0478) = 0.0467.$$

Thus, the continuously compounded rate would be 4.67 percent.

As noted in previous sections, the value of an option is not particularly sensitive to the estimate of the risk-free rate. This outcome is fortunate in the case of real options because there are plenty of other problems to occupy us.

Time to Expiration. Nearly all financial option contracts have a well-defined time to expiration. Although an American-style option might be exercised early, it cannot extend beyond the given expiration date. Real options, however, are not clearly contractual. They involve informal opportunities with sometimes ill-defined expirations. For example, a company might have an option to abandon a project and receive a salvage value, but it may not be clear how long the company can keep the project before abandoning it to claim the salvage value. And it might not be certain how long a company can defer a project and still be able to invest in it, earning the cash flows it originally thought it could obtain.

When projects have uncertain times to expiration, the company will have to recognize, like with some of the other problems described earlier, that either it can obtain a reliable estimate and live with the consequences of errors or it can use more sophisticated models.

Volatility. The volatility in an option-pricing model is one of the most critical variables. In financial option-pricing applications, it is generally the only unobservable variable. That being the case, a major reason why misestimation of a financial option value occurs is because of a difference of opinion on the volatility. In addition, the option price is nearly always very sensitive to the estimate of the volatility. Thus, getting a good estimate of the volatility is critical, which is much easier said than done, especially for real options.

For financial options, generally two approaches can be used for estimating the volatility—historical volatility and implied volatility. The historical volatility approach uses a recent sample of the value of the underlying asset. These values are converted into rates of return, which are simply percentage changes. These rates of return are then converted to continuously compounded rates of return by taking the natural log of one plus the return.[11] From there, one simply estimates the sample standard deviation. If the returns are not based on annual data, and they almost never are, one must annualize the resulting standard deviation.[12]

Option-pricing models require as an input the volatility over the life of the option. Thus, they require a future volatility. Historical volatility is a past volatility. In using it, one is making the assumption that the past volatility can

---

[11]See "Step 3. Value the Option" in Chapter 4.

[12]For details on this procedure, see pp. 189–192 in Chance.

be extrapolated directly to the future volatility, which is rarely the case because volatility frequently changes. Although the past is a good starting point for measuring the future, it should rarely be the ending point.

For real options, past volatility is even more of a problem. Oftentimes, there is no past. A particular project may be entirely new. In some cases, a proxy variable can be used to estimate past volatility, such as the price of a gold mining stock or the price of gold if one is valuing an option to shut down a gold mine. The potential errors, however, are great in using a proxy, and the past volatility derived from a proxy may not be a reliable estimate of the proxy's own future volatility.

The other approach to estimating volatility is the implied volatility. For an option that has an active market, the value obtained from an option-pricing model can be set to the current market value of the option by appropriately altering the volatility. In this way, the market price of the option *implies* a volatility. This approach is an extremely common measure of volatility and indeed of the level of prices in options markets. Unfortunately, it is of almost no use in real options valuation because an actively traded market for the option almost never exists.

So, ultimately, users of real options valuation techniques are forced to estimate the volatility of the underlying project. The literature provides little guidance on this topic and little appreciation for the difficulty of estimating the volatility. But such a problem is not uniquely associated with real options valuation. Suppose a project does not have a real option associated with it. A company would still need to estimate the value of the project using a standard DCF approach. That approach generally involves estimating the cash flows and discounting them at an appropriate risk-adjusted discount rate. For that valuation to be correct, the net cash flow to be discounted should be the expected cash flow. Thus, in order to obtain the expected cash flow, one would have to either estimate probabilities and potential outcomes or make an educated guess at the expected value. Certainly, the former is preferred. But if one can legitimately use estimated probabilities and potential outcomes in a DCF analysis, then one should be able to legitimately use the same information to estimate volatility.

Furthermore, as noted elsewhere in this monograph, the discount rate in a DCF analysis must be adjusted for risk. An appropriate adjustment for risk either comes from a valuation model, such as the capital asset pricing model, or is simply an educated guess. Obviously, the use of a model that attempts to capture the appropriate premium for the level of risk is preferred. But any such model requires an estimate of the volatility or, at a minimum, the same information necessary to estimate the volatility.

If a company does not use probabilistic information in its DCF analyses, it is shooting in the dark in trying to value the underlying project. In that case, the company should forget real options. In fact, it should forget the underlying project as well.

Some Concluding Comments about Inputs. The input requirements for real options valuation are no more stringent than they are for valuing the underlying project itself. If a company is not doing a good job of valuing its projects and those projects do not have real options, then it is not likely to do a good job of valuing those projects if its projects do have real options. If the company has good input information for valuing its underlying projects, it is in a good position to be able to value its real options accurately. Real options valuation does not require more information about the underlying projects than is required for valuing the project in the first place. In some respects, such as not needing a risk-adjusted discount rate, real options valuation requires less information. But that conclusion does not mean that real options valuation proceeds without a hitch. Identifying the exercise prices and expirations of these options is often difficult.

Finally, we should note that, unfortunately, *real options valuation is probably most valuable and most necessary in those situations when it is most difficult to use*. Companies, projects, and options that have less publicly available information offer the greatest potential for earning attractive returns. Yet those are the very situations for which real options valuation is the hardest to use and is the least reliable.

Nontradability of the Underlying Asset

Probably the most critical issue and concern in the area of real options analysis is the assumption that the underlying asset can be bought and sold in a liquid market. Note that we are not just dealing with the question of whether that market is efficient, as discussed earlier; we are dealing with the broader issue of whether a market for that asset even exists and whether one can buy or sell the underlying asset. This problem is important because the option-pricing models on which real options are based are grounded in the idea that the underlying is a tradable asset. As was seen in Chapter 3, when using the binomial approach, the ability to trade the asset and the option in such a manner that no arbitrage opportunity exists is the glue that binds the models together. If the underlying asset cannot be traded, one begins to have doubts about whether the glue is holding.

This problem manifests itself in the form of tracking portfolio limitations and assumptions about hedging, tradability, and risk neutral valuation.

Tracking Portfolio Limitations. A **tracking portfolio** is a combination of traded securities that has the same payoffs as the option. For financial options, constructing a tracking portfolio, at least in principle, is relatively easy. The tracking portfolio normally consists of a leveraged long position in the underlying asset, although it could consist of a leveraged short position. Thus, a particular combination of the asset and debt can reproduce the behavior of the option. The option price then necessarily must equal the value of the tracking portfolio.

It follows that for a real option, the tracking portfolio should be the value of a leveraged position in the underlying asset. But if the underlying asset cannot be traded, does the notion of a tracking portfolio make any sense? In some cases, it does. The tracking portfolio need not always be the exact underlying asset. Suppose the project is a gold mine. A tracking portfolio whose value is driven by the price of gold or the behavior of gold stocks might be sufficient to capture the behavior of the hypothetical tradable asset (the gold mine project). The instrument that serves as such a proxy for the actual asset is called its **twin security**.

But all too frequently, real options problems do not reduce to such simple specifications. The underlying asset often cannot be traded, is highly illiquid, has very high costs associated with trading, is difficult to get a reliable price on because it trades so infrequently, or does not have anything resembling a twin security.[13]

Assumptions of Hedging, Tradability, and Risk Neutral Valuation. We will examine these assumptions of hedging, tradability, and risk neutral valuation with a brief overview of the principle of arbitrage at work. In Chapter 3, we illustrated the simple case of a financial option on a stock worth $100. The stock could move up to $150 or down to $50. The option is a call that allows the owner to buy the stock at $100 one period later.[14] The risk-free rate, r, is 5 percent. The holding period return on the stock if it goes up, denoted as u, is 1.5 ($150/$100), and the holding period return if the stock goes down, denoted as d, is 0.50 ($50/$100). We then computed a variable, p, calculated as

$$p = \frac{1 + r - d}{u - d}$$
$$= \frac{1.05 - 0.50}{1.5 - 0.5}$$
$$= 0.55.$$

---

[13]See pp. 57–58 in Amran and Kulatilaka (1999b).

[14]For a quick picture of this scenario, see Chapter 3, in particular Figure 3.1.

If the stock goes up, the call is worth $50 ($150 stock price – $100 exercise price) at expiration. If the stock goes down, the call expires out of the money and is worth nothing. We then showed that the option price, c, can be obtained by taking the weighted average of $50 and $0, using the weights $p = 0.55$ and $1 - p = 0.45$, and discounting that result to the present:

$$c = \frac{0.55\,(\$50) + 0.45\,(\$0)}{1.05}$$

$$= \$26.19.$$

We will now consider this formula for the price of the option and what it means. First, however, we will segue a little into valuation formulas in general. By definition, the value today of any asset is found by taking its outcomes and weighting each outcome by the probability of that outcome's occurrence. This result is the asset's expected value at a future date. This expected value is then discounted back to the present at a discount rate that incorporates an adjustment for the risk. Consider the stock in this problem. It can go up to $150 or down to $50. We do not need to value the stock; the market has done that for us and has assigned a value of $100. If we know one piece of information, either the probabilities of the outcomes or the discount rate, we can determine the other. Suppose the probability of the up move is 0.6. Then, the probability of the down move is 0.4 and the stock value is obtained as follows:

$$\$100 = \frac{0.6\,(\$150) + 0.4\,(\$50)}{1 + k},$$

where k is the risk-adjusted discount rate. In this problem, a value of $k = 0.10$ completes the equation. If the probability of an up move is 0.7 (and hence a down move is 0.3), then a value of $k = 0.20$ would be correct. If, instead, we knew that k were 0.12, we would have

$$\$100 = \frac{q(\$150) + (1 - q)(\$50)}{1.12},$$

where q is the probability of the up move. Solving for q, we would obtain $q = 0.62$. So, we either need the probability or the risk-adjusted discount rate.

For traded assets, the market does the valuation for us. We do not need to know k or q. But, of course, the investors in the market have to know both k and q. Option-pricing models, however, take the value of the underlying asset as a given; they do not require k and q.

We know that in a market with rational investors, k would have to exceed the risk-free rate. Investors are risk averse, so they require a higher expected return than the risk-free rate. But we will suspend our imagination for a moment and assume that investors, for whatever reason, are not risk averse. Instead, we let them be risk neutral. Risk neutral investors do not worry or even think about risk. They do not require a higher return than the risk-free rate. In that case, notice how they would value the asset:

$$\$100 = \frac{q(\$150) + (1 - q)(\$50)}{1.05}.$$

Solving for q gives 0.55. Notice anything? Here q plays the same role as p in the option-valuation problem. In fact, q is the probability of an up move (and, correspondingly, $1 - q$ is the probability of a down move) if investors are risk neutral. Accordingly, option-pricing models are often said to use risk neutral valuation. Being able to use risk neutral valuation is nice and convenient because then we do not have to worry about estimating actual probabilities of outcomes or how much to adjust the discount rate for risk. We can usually use risk neutral valuation when the underlying is a financial asset and trades in a market where we can observe the value easily and can trade the asset to form a tracking portfolio. But we rarely, if ever, get this privilege in the world of real options.

So, either we have to rescue and justify the notion that the underlying asset in a real option is a traded asset, or we have to discard the notion and simplicity of risk neutral valuation and resort to the necessity of estimating true probabilities and a risk-adjusted discount rate. But before we give up on risk neutral valuation there may be some ways in which we can salvage it.

Copeland and Antikarov's Marketed Asset Disclaimer. Copeland and Antikarov (2001) claim that the project itself, without the real option, can be viewed as a tradable asset. They call this assertion the **marketed asset disclaimer**, or MAD. They argue that if someone is looking for a twin security, that person will select a security that is highly correlated with the underlying project and whose value can easily be obtained from some source. Because the underlying project is perfectly correlated with itself, it meets the correlation requirement for a twin security. Its value is obtainable from standard DCF/NPV analysis. Thus, Copeland and Antikarov argue that the twin security is the project itself.

This approach makes appealing theoretical sense but fails to recognize that the twin security must be a tradable security, one that can be bought and sold at will. In other words, it must meet liquidity requirements and other conditions we discussed earlier. The underlying project does not meet those requirements. But as Copeland and Antikarov note, considering any underlying project without a real option requires making certain assumptions. To obtain a value for any project requires treating the project as though it were a tradable asset. It is well known and widely accepted that the valuation of a project should use standard financial asset valuation techniques. If a company is considering investing $100 million in a plant with a given risk, it must consider that it could otherwise invest $100 million in a financial asset with the same risk. The plant should be valued the same way the financial asset is valued. Moreover, the company's stockholders' claims on the plant are financial assets. Thus, valuation of the plant should proceed as though it were a financial asset.

If the above arguments are accepted, then valuation of the real option should proceed as though it were a financial asset. Using the financial option example just described, an investor should be willing to pay $26.19 for an option that could expire one period later, during which the risk-free rate is 5 percent, with a value of either $50 or $0. The underlying financial asset is assumed to be tradable. If that option represents a real option with those same payoffs in that same interest rate environment, it ought to command the same value. After all, if its value were less, the investor would prefer the financial option; if its value were more, the investor would prefer the real option. Although the forces of arbitrage might not permit the real option value to adjust to that of the financial option value, one can reasonably conclude that opportunities that offer equivalent payoffs should be priced equivalently. In other words, "if it looks like a duck, walks like a duck, and quacks like a duck, it is probably a duck."

Hence, Copeland and Antikarov's marketed asset disclaimer, although perhaps not addressing some important questions, may well be a sufficient argument for dismissing the concern of tradability.

Consistency of All Approaches. One may be tempted to dismiss the risk neutral valuation approach that is the heart of real-option-pricing models, indeed all option-pricing models. Oftentimes, naive users do not see that risk neutral valuation is not hand-waving. But no one is assuming that investors are risk neutral. Rather, risk neutral valuation is simple and imposes only light demands, which is one reason why people work so hard to salvage it.

Risk neutral valuation is not a special or different approach that obtains different numbers from a standard risk-adjusted approach that investors or companies might otherwise use. This argument is illustrated nicely by Feinstein (1999). Consider the following problem involving a deferral option. A company can invest $9 now in a project. One period later, it will learn if the outcome is good or bad. If the good outcome occurs, the company can invest $18 and then begin to generate $10 a year forever, starting one period later. If the outcome is bad, the company can invest $18 and begin to generate $3 a year forever, starting one period later. The probability of a good outcome is

0.6 and the probability of a bad outcome is 0.4. The company has assessed the value of the project using a discount rate of 25 percent. The risk-free rate is 5 percent. Thus, we can obtain the market value of the project in the good and bad outcomes as follows:

$$V_1^G = \frac{\$10}{0.25}$$
$$= \$40$$

and

$$V_1^B = \frac{\$3}{0.25}$$
$$= \$12,$$

where V_1 represents "value" at Time 1 with either the G or B superscript representing the good or bad outcome, respectively. If the company did not have the flexibility to invest, we would assume the company commits to an $18 investment at Time 1. Thus, the market value of the project at Time 1 is specified as

$$X_1^G = \$40 - \$18$$
$$= \$22$$

and

$$X_1^B = \$12 - \$18$$
$$= -\$6,$$

where X_1 represents market value of the project without the deferral option at Time 1 with either the G or B superscript representing the good or bad outcome, respectively. So, with the company committing to invest at Time 1, the project is worth either $22 or –$6. The value of the project at Time 0 is, therefore,

$$V_0 = \frac{0.6\,(\$22) + 0.4\,(-\$6)}{1.25}$$
$$= \$8.64.$$

With the initial outlay being $9, the NPV is –$0.36.

Now, we will value the option to invest using the real options procedure covered in Chapter 3. We need the up and down factors for the value of the project:

$$u = \frac{\$22}{\$8.64}$$
$$= 2.5463$$

and

$$d = \frac{-\$6}{\$8.64}$$

$$= -0.6944.$$

Then, the risk neutral probability is

$$p = \frac{1.05 - (-0.6944)}{2.5463 - (-0.6944)}$$

$$= 0.5383.$$

We next need to identify the values of the options for the good and bad outcomes. If the outcome is good, G, the company makes the investment; the company expends $18 and receives something worth $40. Thus, the option value is $22. If the outcome is bad, B, the company does not make the investment; nothing happens, and the option value is thus zero. So, we can value the option as

$$\text{Value of the option} = \frac{0.5383(\$22) + 0.4617(\$0)}{1.05}$$

$$= \$11.28.$$

Because the company must invest $9 now to obtain this option, it would obviously do so.

As Feinstein shows, we can use a variation of the traditional DCF approach to value this project. We must do so carefully, however, for we cannot simply use the 25 percent project discount rate. The overall project is a blend of the project without the option and the option itself. The discount rate on the option is 5 percent. So, the overall discount rate is a blend of 25 percent and 5 percent.

Recall that once we get out of the risk neutral world, we have to know either the true probabilities of the outcomes or the discount rate. Because we want to know the discount rate, we must know the true probabilities. We already gave them as 0.6 and 0.4. Adjusting Feinstein's approach slightly, the weighted discount rate, k_W, is found as

$$k_w = \frac{\left[qX_1^G + (1-q)X_1^B\right](1+r)}{pX_1^G + (1-p)X_1^B} - 1.$$

Because the company does not invest in state B, X_1^B becomes zero. Thus, in this problem, we have

$$k_w = \frac{[0.6\,(\$22) + 0.4\,(\$0)](1.05)}{0.5383\,(\$22) + 0.4617(\$0)}$$

$$= 0.1704.$$

This result means that if we discount the expected cash flows from the project at 17.04 percent, we will obtain the correct value, and we do:

$$\frac{0.6\,(\$22) + 0.4\,(\$0)}{1.1704} = \$11.28.$$

This rate, 17.04 percent, is a blend of the 25 percent rate on the project and the 5 percent rate on the option.[15]

In other words, nothing about risk neutral valuation, the basis for all option-pricing models, is inconsistent with standard DCF analysis. Although we cannot get to the 17.04 percent rate without resorting to at least some of the assumptions inherent in option-pricing models, we at least know that if we use the correct discount rate, we will be valuing the project the same way we have always valued projects, even long before anyone recognized what real options were.

Alternative Justifications. Finally, we should note that there are other ways in which risk neutral valuation can sometimes be salvaged, even when the assumption that the underlying asset is tradable is clearly not met. Rubinstein (1976) derives a model that shows that all assets in the market can be valued as if they were options. This approach involves the use of risk neutral valuation combined with the assumption that the market portfolio follows a type of joint probability distribution with the underlying asset. Brennan (1979) demonstrates that a risk neutral valuation relationship is appropriate when investors have a particular type of utility function and the return on the underlying asset follows a particular type of distribution, which is normal or lognormal. The conditions that must be met for risk neutrality to hold are not terribly restrictive.

Although these papers are all theoretical and highly abstract, they provide a basis for arguing that a risk neutral valuation relationship is appropriate even when assets cannot be traded. To our knowledge, this point

---

[15]Feinstein shows a different approach to arriving at the weighted-average discount rate and also an approximation method that bypasses the valuation of the overall project. This latter approach allows the user to derive the weighted-average discount rate and use it to value the overall project.

has not been recognized in the real options literature. What it says is simply that in spite of many of the criticisms, limitations, and obstacles we have discussed in this chapter, using option-pricing models to value real options may be acceptable—something that everyone has been doing anyway but apparently without much thought to whether it is appropriate to do so.

Summary

One source of difficulty in applying real options valuation is the use of option-pricing models that make assumptions that may or may not be appropriate in the case of real options. The option-pricing assumptions of lognormality in the distribution of the value of the underlying asset, randomness of prices, and a known and constant volatility of the value of the underlying asset are assumptions that should cause some concern in applying real options valuation. Furthermore, the estimation of inputs, such as the value of the underlying, the exercise price, the time to expiration, and the volatility of the value of the underlying asset, is more challenging for real options than for financial options.

Up until now in this monograph, we have discussed the theory and use of real options valuation and its relevance for financial analysts. An obvious question, however, is whether real options valuation is used in practice and whether observed values of real options can be obtained and compared with values from real options models. In other words, does empirical evidence exist on the use and accuracy of real options models? This question will be answered in Chapter 6.

6. Empirical Evidence on the Use and Accuracy of Real Options Valuation

The literature on real options is replete with theory. Many writers have developed interesting, but usually oversimplified, examples of real options—some taken from their consulting experience. We will take a look at what the empirical research on real options says. In other words, does theory match up with practice?

Direct and Indirect Tests

The studies discussed in this section are either direct or indirect tests of whether the predictions of real options models hold up in practice.

Paddock, Siegel, and Smith. James Paddock, Daniel Siegel, and James Smith (1988) develop a real options model for valuing offshore oil and gas leases in a 1980 federal sale of 21 tracts in the western and central portions of the Gulf of Mexico. Companies buy the rights to drill in certain tracts. Drilling may reveal that oil or gas is present, in which case the company can choose to develop the tract into a well. The authors obtain input data and compare option values with prices at which the tracts were auctioned by the United States Geological Service (USGS). A comparison of prices obtained from real options valuation models with bids placed by companies, as well as estimates obtained from the USGS, provides encouraging but not corroborative results. In other words, real options models were not able to explain the bids as well as one might have hoped. Note, however, that this study was published in 1988, a time when real options theory was not well known, especially by practitioners who would actually use it. In addition, the authors point out that the data provided by the government were not as good as would be hoped or expected in order to carry out a full and accurate real options analysis. Finally, one must take into consideration that when prices are determined by an auction, the "winner's curse" (i.e., a tendency for the highest bidder to pay more than fair value) could explain the discrepancies between the model price and the actual winning bid price. This explanation is consistent with the fact that the winning bids in this auction were higher than the values obtained by the models.

Quigg. Laura Quigg (1993) examines the real option to wait to develop urban land. Specifically, she looks at the market prices of 2,700 land transactions in Seattle during the period 1976–1979 and compares them with prices obtained using a real options model. Her results support the notion that the option to wait and develop land at a later date has value approximately equal to 6 percent of the value of the underlying land. Her results are consistent with predictions from real options models, supporting the belief that investors either use real options models or trade in such a manner that their valuations are consistent with those of real options models.

Bailey. Warren Bailey (1991) tests the effectiveness of real options models by examining the valuation of agricultural companies in Singapore. These companies are well suited for the application of real options models because they produce a very limited number of crops and are traded on the Singapore Stock Exchange, which facilitates the observation of prices and estimation of volatility. Other necessary input data are relatively easy to obtain.

The study covers a period from 1978 to 1985. Discounted cash flow (DCF) analysis and real options models are used to predict the values of seven Singapore companies engaged in the production of rubber and palm oil. In other words, the shareholdings of these companies represent claims on real options and, therefore, should behave similarly to the real options themselves. Both the DCF and real options models give estimates that are consistently low, but the real options model gives estimates that are closer to the market price. Bailey acknowledges the limitations of the real options models and the data, but he argues that he has shown that valuations based on real options theory have significant power over those based on standard DCF analysis.

Berger, Ofek, and Swary. Philip Berger, Eli Ofek, and Itzhak Swary (1996) examine how investors value the option to abandon a company and claim its exit value. The study uses balance sheet information to estimate exit values. Although this study is not as directly about real options as it is about whether investors take exit value into account in valuing companies, some predictions of real options models are relevant to this study. The authors examine a sample of about 1,000 companies during the period 1984–1990. They find a highly significant relationship between a company's market value and its estimated exit value, suggesting that investors take the option to exit into account when valuing companies. They also find that the more likely the option will be exercised, the more valuable is the option.

Hayn. Carla Hayn (1995) examines companies' earnings, focusing on the frequency of and market response to losses. She studies a sample of 9,752 companies for the years 1962 through 1990, analyzing the relationship between earnings, market value, and returns. She finds evidence that investors do not respond to losses to the same magnitude that they do to profits.

Comparing the reaction to losses for companies whose value is above the net liquidation value with those whose value is below the net liquidation value, she concludes that the option to liquidate is valued by investors.

Burgstahler and Dichev. David Burgstahler and Ilia Dichev (1997) examine whether the option to adapt a company's resources to alternative, more productive uses is incorporated in the company's market value. They estimate the adaptation value of a company by relating market value to a company's book value. Using observations on a sample of companies for the years 1976 through 1994, they find support for the idea that the exercise of the adaptation option depends on the level of a company's earnings and its book value; the lower the company's value from the current deployment of assets, the more important the adaptation option.

Moel and Tufano. Alberto Moel and Peter Tufano (2002) study a sample of 285 North American gold mines in the period 1988–1997. These mines are periodically opened and closed, a classic example of the shutdown option discussed in Appendix A. They gather data and test whether these decisions are consistent with the predictions of real options models. The tests support the predictions of the models. Closings are highly related to the price and volatility of gold, the cost of closing a mine, and other factors. Moel and Tufano note, however, that other aspects of mine closings are not captured by the models, such as whether a company has other mines operating.

Clayton and Yermack. Matthew Clayton and David Yermack (1999) use real options models to examine the contracts of major league baseball players. These contracts commonly contain option clauses—in some cases where a team holds the option to extend the player's contract and in some cases where the player holds the option to extend his contract, both for a fixed salary. They examine a sample of more than 1,100 players in the mid-1990s, of which options are contained in about 18 percent of the contracts. Statistical analysis reveals that the predictions of real options models are upheld in these players' contracts. Specifically, option values decrease as a function of the difference between the exercise price and the player's salary (the moneyness of the option) and increase as a function of the time to expiration of the option. Option values, however, are apparently unrelated to the volatility of the player's ability, which is inconsistent with real options models.

The Use of Real Options Models by Practitioners

In the two studies in this section, the researchers have attempted to determine if practicing financial managers recognize and use real options models.

Howell and Jägle. Sydney Howell and Axel Jägle (1997) conduct a laboratory experiment with 82 professional managers of nine companies in the United Kingdom. They ask these managers to answer a series of questions on growth options from some investment case studies. In addition, the authors ask the managers other questions related to their personal situations and the kinds of investment decisions they make in their work. The authors find that these managers tend to value growth options in an erratic manner. This evidence is not consistent with real options theory. These results can be interpreted in two possible ways. The first is that this limited sample of managers is not sufficiently knowledgeable about real options models. The second is that real options models are simply not used in practice. The small sample size, however, is a major limitation of this study. Perhaps a larger sample of managers would produce findings more supportive of real options models.

Busby and Pitts. J.S. Busby and C.G.C. Pitts (1997) conduct a mail survey of senior finance officers in 100 U.K. companies, receiving 44 usable replies. They find that these individuals encounter real options in their work and tend to recognize them. They also find, however, considerable variation in the frequency of encountering real options as well as in how important they perceive real options to be. Most companies do not have procedures in place to identify and evaluate real options, tending to use cruder tools, such as sensitivity analysis. The respondents tend to agree with the predictions of real options models, meaning that the factors that make real options important are indeed perceived in that manner. Interestingly, most of the respondents are not aware of the terminology of "real options" or "growth options," which further suggests that they are unlikely to use the latest knowledge of real options models.

Summary

Data availability is the greatest hindrance to conducing empirical studies on real options, and hence, the body of empirical work on real options is quite limited. Real options necessarily involve private data, often internal and specific to a given company. Even when data are available, accuracy and reliability are in question. Perhaps for that reason, it is all the more remarkable that the empirical work cited in this chapter tends to provide generally supportive evidence. But perhaps that finding is not so unusual. Real options models are based on rational behavior. Even if individual decision makers do not use such models, they still tend to behave rationally. Hence, the models will tend to capture the essential characteristics of real options in the valuation and decision-making process.

Nevertheless, the survey data presented in this chapter do not lend much credence to the belief that managers use or even understand real options. Perhaps this finding is a reflection of the fact that real options theory is relatively young and managers have not been trained to understand it. After all, not until the decade of the 1990s did financial option-pricing theory become widely practiced. Thus, it will likely take longer for real options models to make their way into the toolkit of practicing financial managers. This does not mean that real options models should be abandoned until such time as they are taken up by others. Indeed, using good models before everyone else is an important ingredient in generating value.

7. Summary and Conclusions

The financial analysis of a company is a difficult undertaking, even under the best of circumstances. Financial information is never completely sufficient to uncover the hidden benefits and costs that distinguish one company from another. Even when information is easy to obtain, the analytical techniques often rely on heroic assumptions and forecasts about growth rates, dividend policy, capital expenditures, and a host of other factors that are difficult to predict. Further complicating the process of financial analysis is the fact that many, if not all, companies have some opportunities that are not so apparent. These opportunities are in the form of options that give a company flexibility in making decisions. Companies can terminate projects, switch to alternatives, enter new markets, exit old markets, delay expansions, and expand or contract existing investments. Standard accounting principles do not allow the value of such opportunities to appear on balance sheets, and the gains and losses from changes in the value of these opportunities are never recorded in earnings. Unquestionably, these opportunities are a source of value, but as noted, they are difficult to detect. In fact, we can probably safely say that many companies themselves are unaware of many of these valuable opportunities that they possess.

These opportunities are called real options, named as such because they deal with opportunities related to real investments, as opposed to financial investments. Options on the latter, such as puts and calls that trade on options exchanges and over-the-counter markets and options that are issued by companies to employees and executives, are well known in financial markets. A large body of literature exists on the valuation of these instruments, much of which can be traced to the celebrated Black–Scholes model, for which a Nobel Prize was awarded in 1997. The field of real options analysis has taken its framework from the valuation of financial options and adapted it to real options. Considerable progress has been made in this endeavor; the body of literature on real options is almost overwhelming, although much of it is too complex for practicing financial managers and analysts. In this monograph, we have attempted to glean the most important results from that body of literature and consolidate and condense them into a single document. At the same time, we have added new material on the difficulties of applying real options to real investment problems. In this chapter, we provide a summary of what we have discussed in this monograph.

▨ *Companies are often highly misvalued in the market, with at least a portion of the discrepancy between fundamental values and market values undoubtedly caused by real options.* This phenomenon seems to be particularly evident in the technology industry, where real options are commonly found. Although real options almost surely cannot account for all the seemingly absurd valuations seen in recent years in many technology stocks, they just as assuredly are the source of some of what appears to be overvaluation. Conversely, a failure of the market to recognize real options can mean that some stocks seem undervalued.

▨ *Corporate investment decisions are typically made using standard discounted cash flow (DCF) techniques, which are not equipped to accommodate real options.* When a corporation analyzes a project, it arrives at a net present value (NPV). If this NPV is positive, the project is acceptable. But an NPV analysis is not capable of accommodating the flexibility in many investment decisions. Even something as simple as an option to defer an investment one or more years into the future cannot be easily analyzed using an NPV approach. One can calculate an NPV based on investing today, another NPV based on investing in one year, and other NPVs based on investing in later years. Should the company make the decision of when to invest based on the NPV that is the largest? No. Suppose the largest NPV is associated with the choice of waiting three years. Should the company thus decide today whether to invest in three years? No. What happens if market conditions are not favorable in three years? Real options analysis takes into account the fact that market conditions might not be favorable in three years. The flexibility to forgo investing in three years, if this decision proves to be optimal, is valuable not just in three years but today as well. Real options analysis captures the value of that flexibility today.

▨ *Discounted cash flow techniques that attempt to capture flexibility are not adequate.* Simulation analysis, sensitivity analysis, and decision trees attempt to capture the value of flexibility, but they impose unnecessarily heavy demands on the user, in particular by requiring a risk-adjusted discount rate. How does one go about assessing the risk of an option? It is not the same as the risk of the project itself. Real options analysis assesses the risk of an option the same way that investors assess the risk of the option in an open and liquid market for financial options. Shareholders, after all, can invest in financial options. If real options offer the same payoffs, they should be valued in a similar manner.

▨ *The valuation of financial options has benefited from years of study, evolving from the binomial and Black–Scholes models. These models can be used in the valuation of real options.* Binomial models specify a sequential path of future outcomes for each price of the underlying asset. The option is valued at the expiration at its exercise value. One then steps backward, evaluating at each time point a probability-weighted average of the next two option values at the next time point and then discounting that value back one period at the risk-free rate. The binomial model is extremely flexible and is widely used for valuing complicated options, which certainly describes many real options.

The Black–Scholes model is a mathematical formula that requires five inputs and produces the value of the option. For a real option, the model requires the value of the underlying asset on which the real option is based, the exercise price or amount that must be paid to exercise the option, the length of time before the option expires, the risk-free rate of interest, and a measure of the volatility of the underlying asset.

■ *A number of limitations and difficulties arise in applying real options.* Real options often exist in multiple forms, leading to complicated interaction effects. Real options, indeed all options, are highly sensitive to model risk, which is the use of a wrong model, the use of wrong inputs in the right model, or the incorrect use of a model. Real options are also subject to the criticism that the party that controls the underlying asset also controls the real options. Thus, the underlying asset and the real option can often interact in a manner not built into the models.

■ *Real options models oftentimes do not meet the assumptions inherent in the models.* The prices of the underlying assets rarely adhere to a lognormal distribution and are often not even random, and volatility is seldom known and constant—all violations of the model assumptions. These problems exist to some degree even in financial option applications, but they are much more severe with real options. At the same time, it is not always necessary that the assumptions of a model be met. Many widely used financial models produce reasonably accurate results without conforming strictly to their required assumptions.

■ *The estimation of inputs in real options models is particularly challenging.* The value of the underlying asset is typically measured using DCF analysis, which is subject to considerable sensitivity and the criticism that for real options the underlying asset is not traded in an active, liquid market. In addition, the exercise price is not always easy to identify, particularly given that it is paid at a later date. In some cases, the exercise price can even vary. The time to expiration can even be difficult to estimate. Furthermore, identifying the lives and termination dates of certain options is not always easy. And the volatility is particularly difficult to estimate. Because typically no active market exists for the underlying asset, rarely can one find a set of data from which to estimate the historical volatility, nor can one determine the implied volatility from the prices of actively traded options because these are not actively traded options. Only the risk-free rate is fairly easy to obtain.

   ■ *Probably the greatest criticism of real options valuation is that the models are based on the idea that one can trade the underlying asset and the option to form a risk-free hedge or trade a combination of the underlying asset and risk-free bonds to replicate the payoffs of the option.* Thus, the models require the ability to trade the underlying asset, which is definitely not true for nearly all real options. With this point in mind, this approach to option valuation, called risk neutral valuation, is thought by many to be inappropriate for options. Surprisingly, virtually all of the books and articles on real options dismiss this point. But real options valuation is not dependent on risk neutral valuation and the ability to engage in the hedging and arbitrage as set forth in the models. If real options were valued using DCF approaches with the appropriate risk-adjusted discount rate, they would have the same values as would be obtained using option-valuation methods. Yet, the former approach would impose much greater demands on the user for obtaining input information, such as the risk-adjusted discount rate, than the latter approach. Furthermore, one can easily argue that if real options produce payoffs at their expirations that are like those of financial options, then financial option valuation techniques are appropriate because investors could invest in financial options and receive those payoffs. Finally, risk neutral valuation actually does not impose terribly heavy restrictions on users of the models and can be justified if investors and markets have certain reasonable characteristics. In short, risk neutral valuation, the basis for virtually all financial option pricing models, is actually not a very demanding framework. Indeed, it demands far less than the DCF methods that have been widely accepted for the valuation of capital investment projects that do not contain real options.

   ■ *Empirical research has provided some, but very limited, support for the real-world applicability of real options models.* Some studies have shown that real options in the real world are valued in a manner consistent with real options models, but other studies have not been very supportive of real options valuation. Nevertheless, it is really too early to tell if real options valuation is truly applicable in the real world, because for one, conducting empirical studies on real options is very difficult. The information associated with real options is primarily private information that companies do not generally release. Even when data are available, the data are oftentimes only crude proxies for the key variables. Thus, the studies tend to be subject to limitations associated with having small samples and questionable data. Moreover, the studies do not make clear that managers and investors really understand real options and real options valuation models well enough to incorporate them into the valuation process. Indeed, studies of the knowledge that managers have of real options suggest that managers have much to learn. This finding suggests that real options have a long way to go before managers and investors begin to fully appreciate their true value and are able to properly use and evaluate them.

That real options are not well recognized is no reason to ignore them. Indeed, not understanding a phenomenon that unquestionably exists is all the more reason to learn about it and make use of it as soon as possible. At some time in the not-too-distant future, real options may well be widely understood and properly incorporated into corporate investment decisions and, accordingly, market valuations. Then, the financial world will be high on the learning curve, and the marginal benefits of learning about real options valuation will be much lower. We hope that this monograph has helped the financial analyst gain an appreciation for the potential benefits of understanding real options and a healthy respect for the difficulties and limitations of analyzing them and that he or she will undertake further study of real options while the payoffs from the learning process are still quite high.

Appendix A. Further Illustrations of Real Options in Investment Projects

In Chapter 3 we focused on three types of real options: the growth option, the deferral option, and the abandonment option. In this appendix, we will look at three additional options: the option to default, the **option to contract**, and the **option to shut down**. To illustrate these options, we will use the same capital investment project as depicted in Figure 3.5, adjusting it as needed.

Option to Default

The option to terminate a project at some time during the project's life is called the option to default. By choosing not to invest further and simply dropping the project, the company is, in a way, defaulting, except that no legal implications arise from this type of default. As we discussed in Chapter 3, a default option accompanied by the opportunity to obtain a salvage value from the project is referred to as an abandonment option.

Recall that the initial outlay for this project illustrated in Figure 3.5 is $1,050. We will assume that the company can make an initial investment of $400 with the option to invest the remaining $650 one period later, but this $650 will be increased at the risk-free rate of interest. Thus, the company can invest $650 × 1.05 = $682.50 at Time 1. If the company does not invest the $682.50 at Time 1, the project terminates and no further value is generated.

Recall from the original binomial tree for the capital investment project (Figure 3.5) that at Time 1 the project has a value of either $1,500 or $500. If the project is worth $1,500, the company will certainly invest the $682.50, but if it is worth $500, the company will not invest the $682.50 and will terminate the project. Thus, at Time 1, the values of the project are $1,500 − $682.50 = $817.50 or $0. Using the risk neutral valuation approach, as shown in Chapter 3, we would find the value of the project at Time 0 to be $428.21 as follows:

$$\text{Value of the project at Time 0} = \frac{0.55\,(\$817.50) + 0.45\,(\$0)}{1.05}$$

$$= \$428.21.$$

The company is required to invest $400 at Time 0, so the net present value (NPV) of the project is $428.21 − $400 = $28.21. In this scenario, the project has a positive NPV. Recall from Chapter 3 that the value of the project without the option was –$50. With the option, it is $28.21. Thus, the value of the option is $28.21 – (–$50) = $78.21. This problem is illustrated in **Figure A.1**.

The attractiveness of the project with the option is a result of a combination of the ability to defer the investment and to choose not to invest the remaining initial outlay at Time 1 if the project is not working out. Clearly, this option has value, and in this case, it has enough value to convert the project from an unattractive one to an attractive one.

Figure A.1. Binomial Tree Illustrating the Capital Investment Project with an Option to Default

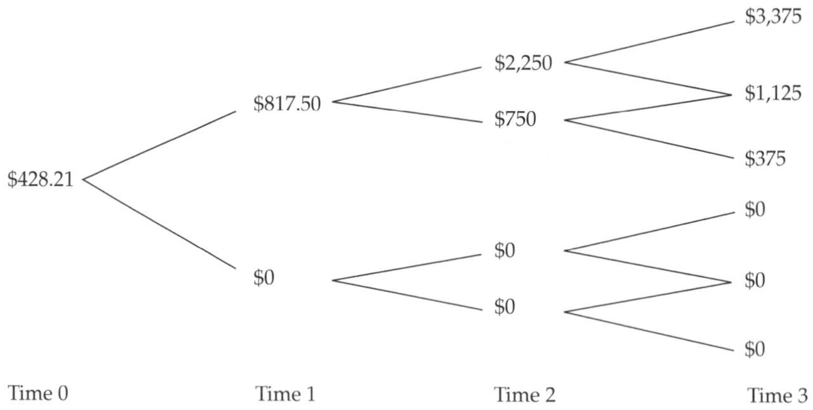

Option to Contract

As with the option to expand that we discussed in Chapter 3, some projects offer an option to contract. This option is combined with an option to defer the initial investment, along with an option to invest an additional sum of money at a later date and reduce the scale of the project. In some ways, this type of option is just the opposite of the growth option. We shall assume that the company must invest $600 now and the remainder one period later. Thus, the amount invested at Time 1 is $1,050 – $600 = $450 increased at the 5 percent interest rate to $472.50. At Time 1, the company is also confronted with an option to invest an additional $40 that will permit it to reduce the scale of the project by half. In other words, by investing some additional money, the company can avoid some of the low cash flows that might occur if things do not turn out as well as hoped. In practice, this situation might correspond to the company incurring some additional costs in order to shut down some of its operations. **Figure A.2** illustrates what happens with this option.

Figure A.2. Binomial Tree Illustrating the Capital Investment Project with an Option to Contract

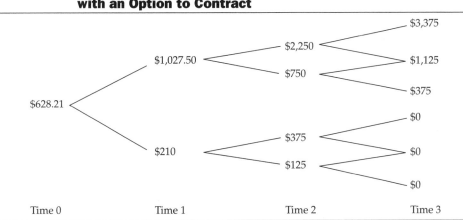

Note that at Time 1 in the top state, the project, which would have been worth $1,500, is now worth $1,027.50. This value reflects the fact that the company must invest $472.50 to continue the project. Thus, it is worth only $1,500 – $472.50 = $1,027.50. Clearly, the alternative of investing $40 more and reducing the scale by 50 percent is not a good idea. In the down state, the project value at Time 1 would be $500 if the company invests the $472.50, so the project would have a value of only $27.50. Alternatively, the company has the option to invest $40 and reduce the scale of the project by 50 percent. So, the project, which would have been worth $500, can be reduced by half to a value of $250 if the company invests just $40 more. Thus, the project would be worth $210 at that point.

At Time 0, the project is worth $628.21 as follows:

$$\text{Value of the project at Time 0} = \frac{0.55\,(\$1,027.50) + 0.45\,(\$210)}{1.05}$$

$$= \$628.21.$$

Because the initial outlay is $600, the project has an NPV of $28.21. The value of the option to contract is, therefore, $28.21 – (–$50) = $78.21.

Option to Shut Down

Most operations incur both fixed and variable costs. Companies often make decisions to shut down operations, thereby saving variable costs. Thus, in some cases, shutting down operations is worthwhile. This situation is perhaps just a slight change from the option to contract; a shutdown is a reduction of 100 percent in scale. We shall, however, introduce another twist, the existence of variable costs and revenues. Specifically, we will change the initial outlay to $750. Think of this outlay as the fixed costs, which are all incurred up front.[1] The company then incurs an additional $100 a year in operating costs if the project is put into production. The project will pay cash revenues of 10 percent of the market value each year. To receive these revenues, the company must incur the operating costs. We also assume that these costs are incurred in order to be able to shut down now *and* open up the next period. Consequently, at Time 3, the company does not incur those costs because it does not open up the next period. If the costs are not incurred, the revenue is lost but the remaining market value applies. In other words, the remaining market value is only 90 percent of what it would otherwise have been had we not introduced this feature.[2]

The nature of this situation is substantially different from the base case where the NPV was –$50. Consequently, we need to establish a base NPV without the shutdown option. **Figure A.3** illustrates the value of the project under the assumption that the company does not have the shutdown option. Time 3 shows the same numbers that came up in Figure 3.5. Time 1 and Time 2, however, have two numbers in each state. The first is the market value of

Figure A.3. Binomial Tree Illustrating the Capital Investment Project without a Shutdown Option

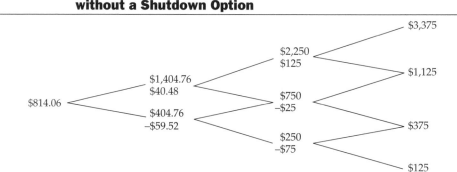

Note: The value of the project is presented at each node with net revenue presented below each value.

---

[1] We could easily spread these costs out over time, but the important point is that the costs are fixed and cannot be avoided.

[2] Revenue paid out of market value corresponds very closely to a dividend if the underlying asset is a stock, although we do add the feature that certain costs must be incurred to pay the revenue and that the revenue is lost if those costs are not incurred.

the project, which is a reflection of its future cash flows. At Time 2, these numbers are the same as the ones in Figure 3.5. In other words, the top number at Time 2 is $2,250 as follows:

$$\text{Value of the project at Time 2 in the top state } = \frac{0.55\,(\$3,375) + 0.45\,(\$1,125)}{1.05}$$

$$= \$2,250.$$

The gross revenue is 10 percent of this amount, or $225. The bottom number in each state at Times 1 and 2 is the net revenue generated by the project, which is the gross revenue minus the $100 operating costs. For the top state, this amount is simply $225 – $100 = $125. Note that the net revenue is negative in the middle state of Time 2, which was obtained as 0.10($750) – $100 = –$25. In other words, business conditions are not sufficiently favorable to justify operations. Right now, however, we are working out the value without the shutdown option. In the bottom state, we also have operating costs exceeding gross revenue.

For the top state at Time 1, we obtain the market value of $1,404.76 from the next two possible values: (1) the net revenue of $125 and the remaining market value of $2,250 – 0.10 ($2,250) = $2,025, for a total of $2,150 in the top state at Time 2, and (2) the net revenue of –$25 and the remaining market value of $750 – 0.10 ($750) = $675, for a total of $650 in the middle state at Time 2. Thus, the calculation is as follows:

$$\text{Value of the project in top state at Time 1 } = \frac{0.55\,(\$2,150) + 0.45\,(\$650)}{1.05}$$

$$= \$1,404.76.$$

For the top state at Time 1 ($1,404.76), the revenue is 0.10($1,404.76) = $140.48. Subtracting the variable costs gives net revenue of $40.48. A similar procedure gives the market value and net revenue in the bottom state at Time 1. At Time 0, we obtain the market value of $814.06 following the same procedure we used to obtain the values at Time 1. Subtracting the initial outlay of $750 gives a positive NPV of $64.06. Although this project is clearly acceptable, it might be even more attractive with an option to shut down and avoid some of the negative net revenues.

Figure A.4 shows the value of the project with the shutdown option. Note that all we have done is replace the negative net revenue numbers from Figure A.3 with zero at Times 2 and 3. By shutting down and avoiding those negative cash flows, the overall value of the project is now higher. Following the same procedure we have previously been using, we find that the value today, at Time

0, is now $862.63. With the initial outlay being $750, the NPV is $112.63. The option value is, therefore, $112.63 − $64.06 = $48.57. The shutdown option clearly has significant value, as is often the case. Companies frequently shut down operations when business conditions are not favorable, so this example is not an unrealistic depiction of a company's option to shut down.

Figure A.4. Binomial Tree Illustrating the Capital Investment Project with a Shutdown Option

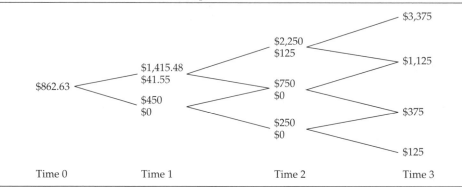

Note: The value of the project is presented at each node with net revenue presented below each value.

Appendix B. Binomial Example of the Hokie Company's Investment Opportunity

In Chapter 2, we examined a company called the Hokie Company, which is considering investing $10 million in a three-year research and development (R&D) program that has a 0.7 probability of leading to a marketable product. If at the end of the third year a product is successfully developed, the Hokie Company must then decide whether to invest $80 million in the production and sale of the product. If the Hokie Company proceeds with this investment, it will generate perpetual after-tax cash flows of $30 million a year with a probability of 0.4 and $15 million a year with a probability of 0.6. The risk-free rate is 4 percent, and the cost of capital is 20 percent. In this application, we shall illustrate the problem with a binomial tree.

In an actual situation, the probability distributions are not likely to be specified in the manner we have done here. The distribution of cash flows if the product is developed is not likely to be as simple as $30 million with a probability of 0.4 and $15 million with a probability of 0.6. Also, the outcome of the R&D process is not likely to be simply a 0.7 chance of developing a product and a 0.3 chance of coming up with nothing. Instead, these uncertainties would be reflected in a measure of volatility. Because the option is whether to invest $80 million in the product, given the success of the R&D process, the volatility is the volatility of the market value of the project. Recall from Chapter 2 that we used a volatility of 0.8. We need to fit a binomial tree to the current value of the project, which we estimated to be $36.438 million. So, we need up and down factors that reflect this volatility. The following formulas give the up and down factors for fitting a binomial tree to a particular situation:

$$u = e^{\sigma\sqrt{T/N}}$$

$$d = e^{-\sigma\sqrt{T/N}},$$

where T is the length of the project and N is the number of binomial periods. In this case, T is 3, representing the three years that the R&D process will take. Because we would like to be able to visualize this project, we shall use only one binomial period; hence, $N = 1$. Thus, the up and down factors are

$$u = e^{0.8\sqrt{3/1}}$$
$$= 3.9974$$

and

$$d = e^{-0.8\sqrt{3/1}}$$
$$= 0.2502.$$

The corresponding binomial tree is shown in **Figure B.1**. Note, however, that these outcomes are not the same as the ones we used in the example in Chapter 2. In fact, in the lower outcome, we previously used a value of zero, representing the case that the R&D process came up with nothing. In this specification, the R&D process comes up with something in both cases, but its market value in one case is extremely small. We would not expect these outcomes to match those we used in Chapter 2. We are laying out a binomial tree of the project's value that is consistent with a three-year life and volatility of 0.80. Indeed, this distribution is likely to be more representative of the actual R&D process and its potential outcomes.

Figure B.1. Binomial Tree Representing the Current Value of the Hokie Company's Investment for One Period
(dollars in millions)

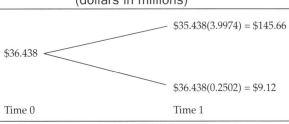

Now we must come up with an appropriate risk-free rate. We originally used 4 percent, but, as noted in Chapter 2, that rate was continuously compounded. A binomial model is a discrete model, so we need a discrete equivalent, which is $e^{0.04} - 1 = 0.0408$, or 4.08 percent. But note that the length of a time step in the tree above is three years. Thus, the risk-free rate over one time step is really $(1.0408)^3 - 1 = 0.1275$, so we must use 12.75 percent.

So, the problem is now set up. The Hokie Company is faced with an option to spend $80 million to obtain an asset that will be worth either $145.66 million or $9.12 million after one time step. If the outcome is $145.66 million, the Hokie

Company will exercise the option and obtain a net value of $145.66 million − $80 million = $65.66 million. Otherwise, the option will expire unexercised. Thus, the Hokie Company faces the outcomes shown in **Figure B.2**.

The question mark represents the project's uncertain value today. To determine this value, we need the binomial probabilities. As shown in Chapter 3, they are obtained as follows:

$$p = \frac{1 + r - d}{u - d}$$
$$= \frac{1.1275 - 0.2502}{3.9974 - 0.2502}$$
$$= 0.2341$$

and

$$1 - p = 0.7659.$$

The value of the option (in millions) is, therefore,

$$\frac{0.2341\,(\$65.66) + 0.7659\,(\$0)}{1.1275} = \$13.63.$$

Note that this value is significantly higher than the value given by the Black–Scholes model of $12.744 million. We would not expect these values to be the same or necessarily close. We mentioned in Chapter 3, however, that the binomial model value converges to the Black–Scholes value with a large number of time steps. Suppose we divide the three-year life into 100 time steps instead of one time step. Of course, we would need a computer to do the calculations, but they are easily programmable. Doing so, we would find that the binomial model value is $12.735 million, which is very close to the $12.744 million we obtained with the Black–Scholes model.

Figure B.2. Binomial Tree Representing the Outcomes of the Hokie Company's Investment for One Period
(dollars in millions)

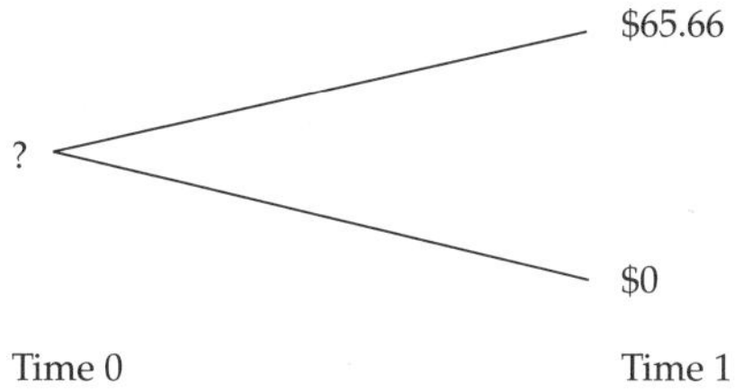

$65.66

?

$0

Time 0   Time 1

Glossary

Abandonment option: The option to cease a project prior to the end of its useful life and to recover the project's salvage value.

American option: An option that can be exercised at any time on or before the expiration date.

Arbitrage opportunity: A market situation in which an asset is priced differently in two markets such that an investor can buy the asset in one market at one price and sell it for a higher price in the other market, thereby capturing the difference in the prices and incurring no risk.

Binomial model: A model for valuing options in which only two possible outcomes or states are associated with the underlying asset for each period of time.

Binomial tree: A graphical representation of a binomial model showing the possible outcomes or states associated with an option and its underlying asset.

Black–Scholes model: A model for pricing options in which the value of an option depends on the value of the underlying asset, the time to expiration of the option, the exercise price, the volatility of the underlying asset, and the risk-free rate or time value of money.

Call option: An option to buy a particular asset at a specified price within a specified period of time.

Compound option: An option to buy or sell an option. That is, the underlying asset of the option is another option.

Decision tree: A graphical representation of decisions and uncertainties over time for an investment project.

Deferral option: The option to invest in an investment project at a later date.

European option: An option that can be exercised only on the expiration date.

Exercise price: The price at which the option allows the owner of the option to buy (in the case of a call option) or sell (in the case of a put option) the specified asset. In the case of a real option, the exercise price is the cost of exercising the option (e.g., the cost of additional facilities in an expansion option). Also known as strike price, strike, or striking price.

Exit value: Salvage value or residual value; the cash flow expected in the future upon disposition of a project's assets.

Expansion option: See growth option.

Flexibility option: An option that provides the opportunity to revise decisions in the future.

Growth option: The option to expand or grow in the future.

Learning option: An option in which the investment in a capital project produces information that reduces the uncertainty regarding future decisions related to the capital project.

Lognormality: An assumption typically used in option valuation that the underlying asset follows a lognormal probability distribution, which implies that the log return on the asset is normally distributed.

Marketed asset disclaimer: The argument that a project can serve as its own twin security that can be used to replicate the option on the project. This argument essentially means that a project can be viewed as a traded asset.

Model risk: The risk associated with using a wrong valuation model, wrong inputs in an otherwise correct valuation model, or the incorrect use of a correct valuation model, which can include programming errors and other mistakes.

Option to contract: The option to reduce the scale of a project.

Option to default: The option to terminate an investment during the time when investment outlays are continuing to be made.

Option to shut down: The option to halt operations, in which this stoppage may be temporary or permanent.

Put option: An option to sell a particular asset within a specified period of time for a specified price.

Real options valuation: The valuation of the options inherent in an investment decision involving a real or intangible asset.

Risk neutral valuation: A process for valuing options based on the assumption that it is impossible to earn a risk-free (arbitrage) profit by trading the option and replicating an offsetting position with a combination of other assets at a price different from the value of the option. This process leads to the result that an option is valued as though investors are risk neutral, even though no assumption is made regarding how investors feel about risk.

Salvage value: The expected value of an asset at the end of its useful life.

Scale-up option: An option that provides the opportunity to expand the capacity of operations.

Scope-up option: An option that provides the opportunity to enter different product lines.

Sensitivity analysis: A technique that allows the examination of the outcomes of an investment resulting from the alteration of one of the variables in the analysis; also known as "what if" analysis.

Simulation analysis: A procedure for determining the value of an investment or option by randomly generating a large set of outcomes according to an assumed probability distribution and averaging the results. Sometimes called Monte Carlo simulation.

Static NPV: The present value of future cash flows of a capital investment less the present value of the capital investment outlay; the net present value in the traditional model of capital budgeting.

Strategic NPV: The sum of the present value of expected net cash flows of a capital project that also accounts for the value of any options associated with the capital project.

Synthetic call option: An investment position that replicates the behavior of a call option, such as a long position in the stock and borrowing.

Tracking portfolio: A combination of traded securities that has the same pay-offs as an option.

Twin security: A traded asset or financial instrument that serves as a proxy for the underlying project.

References

Amran, Martha, and Nalin Kulatilaka. 1999a. "Uncertainty: The New Rules for Strategy." *Journal of Business Strategy*, vol. 20, no. 3 (May–June):25–29.

———. 1999b. *Real Options*. Boston, MA: Harvard Business School Press.

Bailey, Warren. 1991. "Valuing Agricultural Firms: An Examination of the Contingent-Claims Approach to Pricing Real Assets." *Journal of Economic Dynamics and Control*, vol. 15, no. 4 (October):771–791.

Berger, Philip G., Eli Ofek, and Itzhak Swary. 1996. "Investor Valuation of the Abandonment Option." *Journal of Financial Economics*, vol. 42, no. 2 (October):257–287.

Black, Fischer, and Myron Scholes. 1973. "The Pricing of Options and Corporate Liabilities." *Journal of Political Economy*, vol. 81, no. 3 (May–June):637–659.

Bonini, Charles P. 1977. "Capital Investment under Uncertainty with Abandonment Options." *Journal of Financial and Quantitative Analysis*, vol. 12, no. 1 (March):39–54.

Brealey, R., and S.C. Myers. 1996. *Principles of Corporate Finance*. 5th ed. New York: McGraw-Hill.

Brennan, Michael J. 1979. "The Pricing of Contingent Claims in Discrete Time Models." *Journal of Finance*, vol. 34, no. 1 (March):53–68.

Brennan, Michael J., and E.S. Schwartz. 1985. "Evaluating Natural Resource Investment." *Journal of Business*, vol. 58, no. 2 (January):135–157.

Burgstahler, David C., and Ilia D. Dichev. 1997. "Earnings, Adaptation and Equity Value." *Accounting Review*, vol. 72, no. 2 (April):187–215.

Busby, J.S., and C.G.C. Pitts. 1997. "Real Options in Practice: An Exploratory Survey of How Finance Officers Deal with Flexibility in Capital Appraisal." *Management Accounting Research*, vol. 8, no. 2 (June):169–186.

Capel, Jeanette. 1997. "A Real Options Approach to Economic Exposure Management." *Journal of International Financial Management and Accounting*, vol. 8, no. 2 (June):87–113.

Carr, P. 1988. "The Valuation of Sequential Exchange Opportunities." *Journal of Finance*, vol. 43, no. 5 (December):1235–56.

Chance, Don M. 2001. *An Introduction to Derivatives and Risk Management.* 5th ed. Fort Worth, TX: Harcourt College Publishers.

Chatwin, R., Y. Bonduelle, A. Goodchild, F. Harmon, and J. Mazzuco. 1999. "Real Option Valuation for E-Business: A Case Study." In *Real Options and Business Strategy: Applications to Decision-Making.* Edited by L. Trigeorgis. London: Risk Books.

Childs, Paul D., Steven H. Ott, and Alexander J. Triantis. 1998. "Capital Budgeting for Interrelated Projects: A Real Options Approach." *Journal of Financial and Quantitative Analysis,* vol. 33, no. 3 (September):305–334.

Chung, K., and C. Charoenwong. 1991. "Investment Options, Assets in Place, and the Risk of Stocks." *Financial Management,* vol. 20, no. 3 (Autumn):21–33.

Clayton, Matthew, and David Yermack. 1999. "Major League Baseball Player Contracts: An Investigation of the Empirical Properties of Real Options." Working paper, Stern School of Business, New York University.

Copeland, Tom, and Vladimir Antikarov. 2001. *Real Options.* London: Texere.

Dixit, Avinash. 1989. "Entry and Exit Decisions under Uncertainty." *Journal of Political Economy,* vol. 97, no. 3 (June):620–638.

———. 1992. "Investment and Hysteresis." *Journal of Economic Perspectives,* vol. 6, no. 1 (Winter):67–87.

Dunbar, Nicholas. 2000. "The Power of Real Options." *Risk,* vol. 13, no. 8 (August):20–21.

Feinstein, Steven P. 1999. "Toward a Better Understanding of Real Options: A Weighted Average Discount Rate Approach." Working paper, Babson College.

Figlewski, Stephen. 1998. "Derivatives Risks, Old and New." *Wharton-Brookings Papers on Financial Services,* vol. 1, no. 1:159–238.

Grenadier, Steven R. 1995. "Valuing Lease Contracts: A Real-Options Approach." *Journal of Financial Economics,* vol. 38, no. 3 (July):297–332.

———. 1996. "The Strategic Exercise of Options: Development Cascades and Overbuilding in Real Estate Markets." *Journal of Finance,* vol. 51, no. 5 (December):1653–79.

Grenadier, Steven R., and Allen M. Weiss. 1997. "Investment in Technological Innovations: An Option Pricing Approach." *Journal of Financial Economics,* vol. 44, no. 3 (June):397–416.

Hayn, Carla. 1995. "The Information Content of Losses." *Journal of Accounting and Economics*, vol. 20, no. 1 (September):125–153.

Hertz, David B. 1964. "Risk Analysis in Capital Investment." *Harvard Business Review*, vol. 42, no. 1:95–106.

Howell, Sydney D., and Axel J. Jägle. 1997. "Laboratory Evidence on How Managers Intuitively Value Real Growth Options." *Journal of Business Finance and Accounting*, vol. 24, no. 7/8 (September):915–935.

Ingersoll, J., and S. Ross. 1992. "Waiting to Invest: Investment and Uncertainty." *Journal of Business*, vol. 65, no. 1 (January):1–29.

Ip, Greg. 1999. "Analyst Discovers Order in the Chaos of Huge Valuations for Internet Stocks." *Wall Street Journal* (December 27):C1, C2.

Kellogg, David, and John M. Charnes. 2000. "Real-Options Valuation for a Biotechnology Company." *Financial Analysts Journal*, vol. 56, no. 3 (May/June):76–84.

Kemna, Angelien G.Z. 1993. "Case Studies on Real Options." *Financial Management*, vol. 22, no. 3 (Autumn):259–270.

Kester, W. Carl. 1984. "Today's Options for Tomorrow's Growth." *Harvard Business Review*, vol. 84, no. 2 (March–April):153–160.

———. 1993. "Turning Growth Options into Real Assets." In *Capital Budgeting under Uncertainty*. Edited by R. Aggarwal. Englewood Cliffs, NJ: Prentice-Hall.

Kulatilaka, N. 1988. "Valuing the Flexibility of Flexible Manufacturing Systems." *IEEE Transactions in Engineering Management*, vol. 35, no. 4:250–257.

———. 1993. "The Value of Flexibility: The Case of a Dual-Fuel Industrial Steam Boiler." *Financial Management*, vol. 22, no. 3 (Autumn):271–280.

———. 1999. "In Practice: Valuing a New Venture with Real Options Analysis." *CFO Magazine* (November). (See www.cfo.com.)

Kulatilaka, Nalin, and Alan J. Marcus. 1988. "A General Formulation of Corporate Real Options." *Research in Finance*, vol. 7:183–200.

Kulatilaka, Nalin, and Lenos Trigeorgis. 1994. "The General Flexibility to Switch: Real Options Revisited." *International Journal of Finance*, vol. 6, no. 2:778–798.

Leibowitz, Martin L. 1997. *Sales-Driven Franchise Value*. Charlottesville, VA: The Research Foundation of the Institute of Chartered Financial Analysts.

Luehrman, Timothy A. 1998a. "Investment Opportunities as Real Options: Getting Started on the Numbers." *Harvard Business Review*, vol. 76, no. 4 (July/August):51–67.

———. 1998b. "Strategy as a Portfolio of Real Options." *Harvard Business Review*, vol. 76, no. 5 (September/October):89–99.

Magee, J. 1964. "How to Use Decision Trees in Capital Investment." *Harvard Business Review*, vol. 42 (September/October):79–96.

Majd, Saman, and Robert S. Pindyck. 1987. "Time to Build, Option Value, and Investment Decisions." *Journal of Financial Economics*, vol. 18, no. 1 (March):7–27.

———. 1989. "The Learning Curve and Optimal Production under Uncertainty." *Rand Journal of Economics*, vol. 20, no. 3 (Autumn):331–343.

Margrabe, William. 1978. "The Value of an Option to Exchange One Asset for Another." *Journal of Finance*, vol. 33, no. 1 (March):177–186.

Mauboussin, Michael J. 1999. "Get Real." *Frontiers of Finance*, Credit Suisse/First Boston Equity Research, vol. 10 (June 23).

Mayers, David. 1998. "Why Firms Issue Convertible Bonds: The Matching of Financial and Real Investment Options." *Journal of Financial Economics*, vol. 47, no. 1 (January):83–102.

Mayor, Nick. 2001. "Jackpot." *Wilmott*, vol. 1, no. 1 (May):46–53.

McDonald, R., and D. Siegel. 1985. "Investment and the Valuation of Firms When There Is an Option to Shut Down." *International Economic Review*, vol. 26, no. 2 (June):331–349.

———. 1986. "The Value of Waiting to Invest." *Quarterly Journal of Economics*, vol. 101, no. 4 (November):707–727.

Merton, Robert C. 1973. "The Theory of Rational Option Pricing." *Bell Journal of Economics*, vol. 4, no. 1 (Spring):141–183.

Michaels, Daniel. 2000. "For Air France, Sky's the Limit on Growth Potential at Hub." *Wall Street Journal Europe* (May 29):3.

Moel, Alberto, and Peter Tufano. 2002. "When Are Real Options Exercised? An Empirical Study of Mine Closings." *Review of Financial Studies*, vol. 15, no. 1 (March):35–64.

Myers, Stewart. 1977. "Determinants of Corporate Borrowing." *Journal of Financial Economics*, vol. 5, no. 2 (Spring):147–176.

Myers, Stewart, and Saman Majd. 1990. "Abandonment Value and Project Life." *Advances in Futures and Options Research*, vol. 4:1–21.

Østbye, Stein. 1997. "A Real Options Approach to Investment in Factor Demand Models." *Applied Economics Letters*, vol. 4, no. 3:153–157.

Paddock, J., D. Siegel, and J. Smith. 1988. "Option Valuation of Claims on Real Assets: The Case of Offshore Petroleum Leases." *Quarterly Journal of Economics*, vol. 103, no. 3 (August):479–508.

Pindyck, R. 1988. "Irreversible Investment, Capacity Choice, and the Value of the Firm." *American Economic Review*, vol. 78, no. 5 (December):969–985.

———. 1991. "Irreversibility, Uncertainty, and Investment." *Journal of Economic Literature*, vol. 29, no. 3 (September):1110–48.

———. 1993. "Investments of Uncertain Cost." *Journal of Financial Economics*, vol. 34, no. 1:53–76.

Pulliam, Susan. 2000. "Analysts Twist Their Yardsticks to Justify P/E of Cisco & Co." *Wall Street Journal* (April 12):C1, C4.

Quigg, L. 1993. "Empirical Testing of Real Option-Pricing Models." *Journal of Finance*, vol. 48, no. 2 (June):621–640.

Roberts, Kevin, and Martin L. Weitzman. 1981. "Funding Criteria for Research, Development, and Exploration Projects." *Econometrica*, vol. 49, no. 5 (September):1261–88.

Robichek, A., and J. Van Horne. 1967. "Abandonment Value and Capital Budgeting." *Journal of Finance*, vol. 22, no. 4:577–590.

Rubinstein, Mark. 1976. "The Valuation of Uncertain Income Streams and the Pricing of Options." *Bell Journal of Economics*, vol. 7, no. 2 (Autumn):407–425.

Schwartz, Eduardo, and Mark Moon. 2000. "Rational Pricing of Internet Companies." *Financial Analysts Journal*, vol. 56, no. 3 (May/June):62–75.

Shapiro, Alan. 1993. "Corporate Strategy and the Capital Budgeting Decision." In *The New Corporate Finance: Where Theory Meets Practice*. Edited by Donald H. Chew, Jr. New York: McGraw-Hill.

Stonier, John. 2001. "The Change Process." In *Real Options*. Edited by Tom Copeland and Vladimir Antikarov. London: Texere.

Titman, S. 1985. "Urban Land Prices under Uncertainty." *American Economic Review*, vol. 75, no. 3 (June):505–514.

Tourinho, O. 1979. "The Option Value of Reserves of Natural Resources." Working Paper 94, University of California at Berkeley.

Triantis, Alexander. 1999. "The Hidden World of Real Options." *Risk*, vol. 12, no. 10 (October):52–54.

Triantis, Alexander, and J. Hodder. 1990. "Valuing Flexibility as a Complex Option." *Journal of Finance*, vol. 45, no. 2 (June):549–565.

Trigeorgis, L. 1988. "A Conceptual Options Framework for Capital Budgeting." *Advances in Futures and Options Research*, vol. 3:145–167.

———. 1991. "A Log-Transformed Binomial Numerical Analysis Method for Valuing Complex Multi-Option Investments." *Journal of Financial and Quantitative Analysis*, vol. 30, no. 3 (September):309–326.

———. 1993a. "The Nature of Option Interactions and the Valuation of Investments with Multiple Real Options." *Journal of Financial and Quantitative Analysis*, vol. 28, no. 1 (March):1–20.

———. 1993b. "Real Options and Interactions with Financial Flexibility." *Financial Management*, vol. 22, no. 3 (Autumn):202–224.

———. 1996. *Real Options: Managerial Flexibility and Strategy in Resource Allocation*. Cambridge, MA: MIT Press.

Trigeorgis, L., and S.P. Mason. 1987. "Valuing Managerial Flexibility." *Midland Corporate Finance Journal*, vol. 5, no. 1 (Spring):14–21.

Selected AIMR Publications

Benchmarks and Attribution Analysis, 2001

Best Execution and Portfolio Performance, 2001

Core-Plus Bond Management, 2001

Currency Risk in Investment Portfolios, 1999

Developments in Quantitative Investment Models, 2001

Ethical Issues for Today's Firm, 2000

Evolution in Equity Markets: Focus on Asia, 2001

Fixed-Income Management for the 21st Century, 2002

Frontiers in Credit-Risk Analysis, 1999

Global Bond Management II: The Search for Alpha, 2000

Hedge Fund Management, 2002

Investment Counseling for Private Clients II, 2000

Investment Counseling for Private Clients III, 2001

Investment Firms: Trends and Issues, 2001

Organizational Challenges for Investment Firms, 2002

Practical Issues in Equity Analysis, 2000

Risk Management: Principles and Practices, 1999

The Technology Industry: Impact of the Internet, 2000

A full catalog of publications is available on AIMR's World Wide Web site at **www.aimr.org**. You may write to AIMR, P.O. Box 3668, Charlottesville, VA 22903 U.S.A.; call 434-951-5499; fax 434-951-5262; or e-mail **info@aimr.org** to receive a free copy of our product catalog. All prices are subject to change.